VOICES

VOICES

*The stories of four
troubled teenagers
as told in personal
interviews to*
BEATRICE SPARKS

Times
BOOKS

Manufactured in the United States of America. Published simultaneously in Canada by Fitzhenry & Whiteside, Ltd., Toronto.

Designed by Beth Tondreau

Library of Congress Cataloging in Publication Data

Sparks, Beatrice Mathews.
  Voices.

  1. Youth—United States—Attitudes—Case studies. 2. Conflict of generation—Case studies. 3. Interpersonal communication.
  I. Title.
HQ796.S64   301.43'15'0922   77-79044
ISBN 0-8129-0729-9

To the real Mary, Mark, Millie and Jane

Acknowledgment

My deepest thanks to four young friends, called Mary, Mark, Millie and Jane in this book. Each trusted me enough to share with me their most intimate and sometimes hurting thoughts and remembrances, in the hope that those experiences would help other young people make wiser decisions and value judgments in their own lives.

All four case histories are published with permission. In each case names and essential facts have been disguised.

Contents

Introduction

Since 1955 I have been working with kids who have problems. I have found them in many places: At the Youth Center Division of the Utah Mental Hospital where I was a music therapist, at Brigham Young University where I taught special classes, and at many seminars and youth conferences where I have lectured. I have interviewed them in connection with books and articles I have written. "Hurting kids" are everywhere!

During the summer of 1975 I began extensive interviewing to look into the problems of youth, spending much time at Focus, a runaway house in Las Vegas, Nevada.

In the fall of that year my husband and I traveled by car from San Francisco to New York, taking a northern route, and returning via Los Angeles on a southern route. This entire trip was devoted to interviewing young people. The following year we traveled to Texas for more interviews.

In all I talked with well over one thousand young people in sixty-seven cities and towns in twenty-five states. Sixteen of these cities had populations of 200,000 and over, twenty had populations of 40,000 to 200,000, and sixteen towns had populations from 10,000 to 40,000. There were fifteen towns with populations under 10,000.

With the assistance of teachers, counselors, and the kids themselves, I endeavored to interview a balanced number of "privileged," "underprivileged," "soshes," "sleazes," and "inbetweens," but this presented no problem as each township, city, and school has its distinct caste system. These castes nearly always have their own hangouts—they work, study, and date at different places.

Each young person, before being interviewed, obtained a signed release from a parent or guardian granting permission for my use of the interview material providing I changed names and places to protect the identity of the person concerned. Parents and teachers never saw the interview material, which allowed the kids to speak frankly and sincerely.

Kids were always anxious to talk, actually hungry and eager to have someone who sincerely wanted to "listen" and "not hurt." There were always more kids lined up, many more willing to cooperate than I could use. All were looking for answers, for a chance to help themselves and other kids. I found a rapport so deep and stable and caring among them that I wished the thoughts they shared with me could be shared with all people, mainly to let adults see how sensitive young people are and how deeply they can "hurt." And to let young people see that they are not alone in their frustrations and fears.

Chapter 5 provides a flashback to the four young people who tell their stories in this book. It provides clues to how they, individually, could or could not face and overcome their problems. In each case many cries for help, love, and acceptance are all too evident.

I chose cults, suicide, homosexuality, and peer pressure as the main themes of *Voices* because I believe they, plus drugs and liquor, are the biggest and the most "now" problems young people have to face. There is no running away from them! These problems, in varying degrees, are in every school from Hong Kong to Kalamazoo to Phoenix. We cannot isolate kids from them; we can only hope to educate them so they will accept as a privilege their right to free agency and will take responsibility for their own actions, and will make intelligent decisions concerning their own lives.

Beatrice Sparks
Provo, Utah

VOICES

MARY
the cult experience

Life is so plastic, so plastic, meaningless and worthless . . . the apartment we live in with its wood and glue chairs and its plastic covered furniture and my plastic Mom and Stepdad. Actually, each is like two people; at home, working automatically, cleaning, shopping, cooking, and sitting like lumps in front of the boob tube; but the minute it's time for them to *go out* that door, they get cleaned up and dressed up—sparkling and tinkling, and they turn on the personality and the energy and the pizazz. When I go to either one of their offices for something, it's as if I don't even know them. They treat me differently, with life and respect as if I'm important. It's like everything is important there, but not at home! When they open *that* door, they shed all their animation with their coats and just become colorless, uncaring, and unfeeling blobs. I can't believe it! Once in a while I go to lunch with one of them, or occasionally both, and we talk and laugh like life has meaning; but, man, within the four walls of what we call "home," it's nothing . . . cold, unimportant existence! The only time they get excited enough even to seem human is when I don't clean my room or do some of the menial, unimportant things I'm supposed to do.

They're turned off about everything, but . . . well, with my Mom it's women's lib. She wants Frank to do as much around the house as she does, and she wants to be as important and looked up to and respected, and all that junk, in her office as he is in his; and she wants as many women as men in government and executive positions. She fights me to be an A student so I can head a General Motors or an IT&T. Actually, sometimes I think the whole setup is a farce with women wanting only the Amazon-type race to come back. Often I wonder what would have happened if Mom had had a boy baby instead of me. Would she have hated him? Or resented him, or treated him like an inferior as she does my step-Dad, Frank? Oh, maybe not really an inferior but certainly not anybody important. And Frank, he's only interested in beer and sports on TV. Other programs he tolerates, but that's the way he handles everything in our little inside-locked-up gray-nothing cocoon.

At school it's just more of the same. Everybody doing only what they have to do, not with joy and anticipation and healthy competition, but just barely doing what barely has to be done.

I have to cut through a park to get home and often I think about my future and hope that there really is more to life than this. I wonder if this busting-out type yearning is only within my heart and my soul, if I have one. Do I really have one? I wish I had someone who could explain these feelings and needs, someone who would want to.

One bright, sprouting spring day I felt so happily explosive inside I even brought those concepts home and tried to get Mom and Frank to talk about them . . . what was life really all about anyway? But they were having early TV dinners on TV tables in front of the ever-turned-on TV set. It was their God, they worshiped it and reverenced it and nothing else in life was important.

The news was on. It was about starving children in the world—wan little faces and bony little bodies, huge staring eyes popping out of pathetic little faces, eyes that pleaded and begged for food and caring and compassion; but neither Mom nor Frank were truly tuned-in even to that. Somehow their circuits seemed just to go through the set and turn back into themselves, their needs, their desires.

The tiny dark faces on the screen made hard

knots in my stomach, made me feel that I wanted to throw up, that my eating anything ever again would somehow deprive them, but Mom and Frank didn't miss a trip with their forks between their tin TV pans and their mouths. Those children weren't real, I wasn't real, nothing was real. I didn't want to be like that! I couldn't be like them! I wouldn't! But what else was there for me? For anyone?

I was in my second year of high school, and it was a drag, a big, boring, nothing, gray plastic drag. Occasionally I went out with boys or girls, but even that was a drag. All the guys seemed really interested in was sex and booze and pot; the girls the same, plus all the other negatives of the world. I wondered if there were other kids who had the same feelings and needs I had.

I'd always been a kind of loner. I'd never really been able to trust people completely; in that sense maybe I was more plastic than my parents. I began to wonder what was really inside all my peers. Life became more and more lonely. I became more and more confused and the burning need inside me more intense. I retreated into my studies, but there had to be more to life than getting A's in Spanish and biology, or working as assistant editor on the school paper. I had to find it. I approached Mom and Frank about buying a little house so we could have a yard. I promised I'd take care of it and supply not only our flowers, but our vegetable needs. They laughed at me. They couldn't comprehend why anyone would want to take on more "useless" responsibility and expense than they had to. I tried to explain that intangible something inside me that cried out for . . . for just more than we had in our lives; but they weren't listening, or at least they weren't hearing.

The next few weeks were all downhill. Then one day when I was at my lowest ebb, I sat on the bus next to a nondescript young person who seemed to sense my loneliness and confusion. She reached over, touched my arm to get my attention, and looking me straight in the eyes, said gently and without a flinch of self-consciousness, "Jesus loves you."

It was as if someone had turned up the furnace on a cold day, or turned on a welcome light during a night filled with nightmares and darkness, or rescued me just before I was going over Niagara Falls. I didn't know what to say or how to act. She just smiled. "Doesn't it give you a warm, secure feeling to know that Jesus really does care about you, and about me, too?"

Words started tumbling out of my mouth, all the questions, and longings and unfulfillments that had been harassing my life. It was amazing how many answers she had, and they all seemed to stem back to Jesus. I felt happy but a little

7

embarrassed. I had always been taught that religion was sort of a crutch used by weak people. It was something to kind of snicker at like country music with all its inarticulate, ungrammatical, backward devotees, something connected with Negro spirituals, and Oral Roberts' superstitious "faith healing" and all that psychosomatic stuff. I wanted to laugh and turn away from her, but I couldn't. What she was saying was so simple and so fulfilling I wanted it to be true. I wanted it to fill up all the gaps, supply all the answers. I missed two stops.

The girl said she'd meet me the next day in the public library conversation room. I could hardly wait. It was like being at the beginning of the yellow brick road leading to Oz or something else as magical and wonderful.

That night Frank was in an automobile accident. Coming home from the bowling alley, he was hit head-on by a bunch of drunk kids. The doctors said he wasn't too seriously hurt, but his face looked like hamburger. It was the first time I'd ever seen Mom pay any real attention to him, and I guess I felt more sorry for her than for him. She needed him so, wanted him so; I guess she always had and maybe hadn't even known it herself until she almost lost him. She, who'd always wanted to be number one in the house and in her own life as well as in everybody else's, now cried out to him about how she wanted to change her priorities; rather she cried out to me, because we had to sit in the little alcove outside his room. I felt guilty about doubting her sincerity, but something inside me kept insisting that as soon as he was well everything would go back to the old status quo.

I felt deep misery about not being able to meet the Jesus Freak and find out their theory about the wonders of life and the universe, but I kind of shrugged it off. She, too, was probably putting me on. The reason I had listened so intently and wanted so much to believe what she had said was merely because she was saying what I had been wanting to hear—that somehow, somewhere, life was easy and simple, with no battles to be fought, no decisions to be made, no problems to be solved. Utopia! That was for fools and morons! I'd been well-schooled by my Mother to know education and aggressiveness were the answers, not escape and subservience.

It was almost time for school to let out for the summer, and I was glad because life was really beginning to overpower me. School was a big phony baloney hassle with the inmates running the asylum: teachers and principals and counselors afraid of the kids and of each other, afraid of the School Board, the State Board, the government. Students intimidated by their peers, disrespected by their teachers, suffocated by their social and home life-styles and pressures. We were all like a bunch of lost souls—looking, searching, yearning, waiting for a Pied Piper to come and spirit us away to a better today, a better tomorrow. One by one we had rooted out possibilities that weren't answers; a few years back doping had seemed like the answer, but it wasn't, then alcohol, then sex, but none of them filled that lonely, empty gap, that big vacant hole in most of our lives.

On the first day of June at exactly 2:00 P.M. (I knew because the bell in the tower was ringing), I met Dawn, a clear-eyed, quiet, smiling girl who said exactly the same thing to me that a few weeks before the other weird Jesus Freak had said: "Jesus loves you." Then she added, "unconditionally."

It about blew my mind because at that positive moment I needed to feel someone loved me, someone *cared about me!* Not just someone to feed me, to clothe me, to put a roof over my head, and correct my grammar and diction and climb the wall when I didn't get straight A's in school, or when I used language every other kid in the whole world probably used with impunity.

Actually, it was even more than what Dawn said. There was something reassuring about her simplicity, something that bred confidence and security. Together we walked to the park where we rapped for hours.

Dawn was like me; she had been caught up in the rat maze of existence, exposed to selfishness, apathy, and superficial floating with no hopes or dreams or possibilities for a brighter tomorrow.

The sun was sinking, but I didn't want to leave. I didn't know how I could feel so close to someone when we had just met. Dawn was like the blood sisters I had never had. She warmed me with her presence and made me feel secure and important. I longed to ask her home but I knew Mom would never understand or accept that because she . . . well, she wasn't dressed, to quote Mom, "like she was somebody." People according to Mom had to "look like they were someone before they could actually be someone."

I had never really felt before that I belonged, but with Dawn, I did! It sounds dumb but we were one, we thought like one and hoped like one and looked forward to and wanted the very same things out of life. Simplicity and security and peace and love and understanding. Both of us talked at once trying to share our concepts and always they were identical. We didn't want competition, where we had to walk on others to win or even exist. We didn't want anger or violence or hostility. We wanted love and security and everybody taking care of everybody else. Just talking about these wonderful concepts made my heart sing inside me until it felt like a caged bird.

Suddenly Dawn said she had to leave because the van was picking her up by the post office. She invited me to go with her. It was like being invited to go to Never Never Land with Peter Pan or Over the Rainbow with Judy Garland or to follow that Pied Piper I'd dreamed about. All the sunshine and joy within me broke loose enveloping me in a kind of excitement and wonder that I had always felt had existed but I had never actually enjoyed before.

I thought only once about Mom and Frank, and then only that their lives would be more adjusted to their own nothingness without me than with me. I was the only thing that ever seemed to upset the quiet grayness in their dull Garden of Eden, practically the only thing they ever lost their control about or raised their voices over. All of us would be better off. Dawn suggested I call and leave a message at Mom's office so she wouldn't think I'd been kidnapped or murdered or something.

I told Dawn I had only about seven dollars in my purse, but she said money was not important. Imagine, going into a life where material things were not first, first, first on the list of priorities, and where trying to walk on and scramble over people to get to the top of the class, or the top job, or the top anything wasn't the main line of business! I could hardly stand the ecstasy of it.

As soon as we were in the van, everyone greeted each other with "Jesus loves you." Not just a superficial how-do-you-do type of "who cares?" but a friendly, sincere statement of truth. At least something inside me wanted to believe that it was truth. I'd never had too much to do with anything of a religious nature except in a light vein before.

Someone started singing, "Jesus loves you, this is true, and He wants to help you, too. Lift your arms and heed His call. He is calling, calling all. Say you love Jesus. Say you love Jesus. Say you love Jesus and feel the joy that brings."

I started singing with them. They repeated the little song over and over, and I really could feel joy building inside. It reverberated from the front to the back and from one side of the bus to the other. We were all singing and shouting and hugging each other in a trusting, brotherly oneness as if we had all known each other forever. The bus, which was about half-full when it stopped for us, stopped at another five or six places and picked up more kids until we were all practically sitting on each other's laps. I'm sure there were about fifteen of us in a little bus that probably should have held eight or ten.

I remembered having this same type of camaraderie once on a YWCA holiday. We were only little kids, but with our leader we'd laughed and joked and sung. This was more serious and yet it wasn't. We were singing songs about Jesus and love and belonging and doing chants and stuff together. I couldn't get over how we all seemed as one. There wasn't any obvious leader, but what one started we all became a part of.

Once a boy started clapping his hands in rhythm and saying: "who" . . . clap, clap . . . "do" . . . clap, clap . . . "we" . . . clap, clap . . . "love?" clap, clap. Everybody raised their arms and waved them, wildly shouting . . . "Jesus, Jesus . . . Jesus Christ of Nazareth, Jesus Christ our Savior," or anything else they felt compelled to say. I joined them. The words seemed to come out automatically.

It was like a school cheer or some kind of new high. I didn't want it to wear off ever . . . ever . . . ever . . .

Someone started chanting, "I was sad . . . I was alone . . . no one cared . . . no one understood." Almost in unison the whole bus started singing: "Jesus cares. He would have come to your aid . . . if you had prayed." A girl's voice from somewhere back in the darkness cried: "I was lonely . . . I was afraid." Again the group sang, "Jesus cares. He would have come to your aid . . . if you had prayed."

Another voice: "My boyfriend dumped me . . . I was lost . . . I wanted to commit suicide." The voices: "Jesus cares. He would have come to your aid . . . if you had prayed."

I couldn't believe my ears when I heard my own voice hoarsely whispering, "I was less than nothing . . . I was a plastic person . . . no goals, no purpose, no real reason for existing."

The voices sounded like an angelic chorus and they enfolded me. "Jesus cares. He would have come to your aid . . . if you had prayed." I started weeping—coarse, wracking sobs that billowed tears out of my eyes and wiped the meaningless-ness out of my life. Dawn put her arms around me and hugged me with a compassion and under-standing that made me never, ever, ever want to leave her or this new . . . whatever I had found.

I half-slept and had the same wonderful, com-forting, protecting feeling I remembered having once when I had been, oh, maybe three or four years old. We had been driving over a long, hot desert road, my real Daddy and Mama and me. I had sat between them with my head in Mama's lap and my thumb in my mouth, with my ragged but cherished, soft security blanket clutched tightly in my little fist, feeling like a cat sounds when it purrs. I felt the same kind of comfort and belonging now, a feeling I thought I'd never experience again. And I didn't want to wake up, ever. It was too wonderful. I felt protected and comforted and, well, sacred. Imagine me, the carefully reared atheist feeling so . . . I pushed the thought of my past out of my mind.

The sky was just becoming gray when we reached our destination. It was someplace out in wooded country, and the big old house nestled back in the shadows seemed rooted and protective. Then suddenly it took on the characteristics of all the shacks I had seen on TV and in movies where hippies go. What if I was getting myself into something I couldn't get out of? A commune where . . . a jumbled, confused picture of wild drug orgies and sadism and slavery rose in my mind, and fear clutched and grabbed at me.

Dawn seemed to read my mind because her arms went around me again. "It isn't anything like that," she said. "You'll find only peace and love and harmony and belonging. You'll love it, you'll love it, you'll love it. And Jesus and all of us will love you.

"It's really a tiny glimpse of heaven on earth," she whispered in my ear. "Haven House will prepare you to live in the real Heaven that comes after this life."

She said it so sincerely and so believingly that

the doubt that had started to pass through my mind was wiped out, especially when, one by one, the group started singing, so softly they were almost a part of the whir of the motor and the drumbeat of the wheels as they throbbed over the long, bumpy dirt road leading up to the house. Two welcoming lights were shining in the windows. One by one as kids woke up they joined the singing: "Welcome to our Jesus home. He is there to meet you. You'll be safe and cared for there. He'll be there to greet you. Oh such love, oh such love, oh such love and caring. Oh such love, oh such love, oh such love and caring. You'll be safe. You'll be safe. You'll be safe and cared for."

The bus almost bounced off the road as everyone shouted at the top of their lungs, "I'm coming, Jesus. I'm coming, Jesus! I'm coming home, Jesus!"

It was not until we were off the bus and running around in special little formations that I realized almost half the kids were newcomers. We were dressed differently, and there was something more uptight and untrusting about our mannerisms, but we didn't have much time to compare our backgrounds or reasons for being there or anything because everything was so structured. After about fifteen minutes of a kind of calisthenics where we all stretched out our arms and cried, "I'll reach out to Jesus," and then lifted up our arms and shouted, "I'll reach up to Jesus," we reached down and vowed, "I'll pick up people who are down and out and bring them up to Jesus."

We were herded inside and sat cross-legged on mats in a big bare room, which had obviously been made by tearing out two partitions. Everything was either painted or covered in shiny white or the brightest of yellows. There wasn't any coordination or balance to any of it, and my Mother would have hated it, but even the haphazardness of it seemed to have a special meaning to me.

It was as if it had grown without pressure or contemplation or thought, just a natural process.

We sang a thank-you song for everything we could think of. We were all like clean, fresh little children learning appreciation and gratitude with everything kind and simple and good. Each person as we went around the room supplied a word, and the simple song was repeated over and over as we all realized we were grateful for the same things. If the new ones were like me, they had never thought about these things before.

Thank thee, Jesus, for the air, for the blessed gift of air.
Thank thee, Jesus, for the sun, for the blessed gift of sun.

Thank thee, Jesus, for my health, for the
special gift of health.
Thank thee, Jesus, for my mind, for the special
gift of mind.

We went on through food, clothes, flowers,
trees, grass, music, color, and everything until we
all realized there was no possible way we could
ever be thankful enough for all the wondrous
blessings we were gifted with. Few of us had
rarely even thought about them, to say nothing of
being appreciative.

Then Trust came in; that was his name. He
explained how we had been conditioned in our
outside lives to put importance on the wrong
things, and he told us how here in our new "gno-
lum" we would learn to respect and really enjoy
ourselves, our surroundings, and our eternal
growth patterns. Here we would find content-
ment.

He seemed to be looking directly at me, almost
through me, checking my mind, my own personal
needs, and he assured me there would be mental
and emotional stimuli far beyond my greatest ex-
pectations, and that I would not stagnate mentally
in the slightest degree. Closing his eyes for a moment, he quoted from Shakespeare and Albert
Einstein. I could hardly contain my rapture. I

would have it all, all life had to offer. I really would!

A slight hush fell over us. I felt a shiver of awe pass through me as the room's lights seemed to brighten, and Sky was introduced. I wondered if it was some kind of theatrical trick, or if the sun had just happened to come out from behind a cloud as he entered the room. Or maybe the background stereo that had begun to play hosanna-type music when he entered had affected my reality. Whatever, he was magnificent, dressed all in white, with his hands held out in a simple show of love and acceptance that was really beautiful to behold.

Five other people followed behind him. They, too, were dressed in white. Their faces were gentle with compassion and caring, and again, a feeling of protection and oneness radiated from them to me until it was almost a tangible thing.

By now it was obvious which of us were the seven new ones, for we stumbled over the patterns. But even when we failed, no one condemned or criticized. It was as if we were children being led by the hand into a wonderful new world. Those already familiar with the surroundings loved us and wanted to help. Everything was much bigger than physical needs, which didn't seem important. There was only our singing and praising as we, both in spoken word and song, gave "Glory to Jesus our King. Hosanna to our Messiah, who will save and lead us from sin into worlds of happiness reserved only for Him and His special chosen few followers."

My spine tingled. Was I to be one of the chosen few? What had I ever done to deserve such a blessing? How had His followers ever found me? What had led them to me and me to them? I couldn't believe the wonder of it! It was a spiritual experience, the kind of thing I had laughed about in the past. I felt the wetness of tears as they streaked down my cheeks. How guilty and unworthy I felt—I, who had always been the first to make snide remarks about Jesus Freaks and "getting religion." Could I ever be forgiven for my ignorance, for my lack of understanding, for my stupid superiority in placing importance on the wrong things? Only a day ago I would have scoffed about all the feelings I was now experiencing. How superficial I had been, how misguided and disillusioned.

Sky walked through the room and touched my head. It was like an electric shock, something literal and powerful.

Each of us new ones stood to tell how we had been led to Haven House—how helpless and lonely and lost we had felt on the outside and how in tune and protected we now felt.

Four long prayers were said by Sky and two of

his followers; then we were told we would begin a fast so we would be worthy to be baptized, or buried into the waters of death, to come up out of those waters born again and ready to receive a new name and become a new, reborn person.

The thought flicked through my mind that I hadn't eaten or drunk anything for almost twenty-four hours as it was, but I shrugged it off. If the others could stand it, I could. Trust passed around little T-shaped sticks, just tall enough to come about to our chins while we sat cross-legged on the floor. I saw the older members lean their arms or chins on them and I followed. It seemed quite comfortable.

Sky began a long discourse about life before this life and life after this life. It was exhilarating, fascinating; but after a couple of hours I found it very difficult to stay awake or comprehend it any more. Each time I felt myself drifting off, some-one reached over and touched me, or poked me or pinched a very sensitive nerve in my neck. In a way I appreciated it because I didn't want to miss a thing; in another way I felt I would literally die if I couldn't soon straighten my legs and stretch my body. I had never had such severe cramping aches before in my whole life; yet I felt that if all the others could take it, certainly I could. Also, I had to go to the bathroom so badly, I thought my kidneys would burst. But I couldn't be the first to give in to physical needs. I couldn't and I wouldn't!

At the end of three and a half hours of sitting in a position most foreign and uncomfortable, Sky told us we had only one more half hour to go to prove our mastery of mind over body. I wanted to scream with the pain shooting up from just below my right knee through my thigh and I wondered if I could ever bear it. What if I got a blood clot, or the circulation had ceased and I'd get gangrene or something? Then I knew nothing bad would happen because Sunshine had started talking about the power of mind over body and how she had been a weak little diabetic when she first met Jesus. She talked about the mental, spiritual, and physical health and strength she now had, how she now controlled her destiny as well as her body functions and how we all could, too, with a little faith and a lot of discipline. Her talk made me feel weak and foolish. If I couldn't control my kidneys, how could I ever hope to control anything else in the universe? But try as I would, I could not, and felt a little puddle of water seep through my pants. I wanted to cry and explain that it had been way over twenty-four hours, and that I . . . but the others had probably gone almost that long and they . . . I was a weak, stupid failure and probably would be the only one who couldn't stand even the smallest amount of pressure and stress.

Someone began singing, "We'll walk in the steps of our Master, We'll do what He wants us to do. Through testing and proving and trials, We'll rise with the glorious few." My legs and feet and back and neck no longer ached, and I felt I could sit there through the rest of eternity. But it was time to get up and walk through the woods, emptying our bladders, then slowly taking time to smell each flower. We felt the black, moist earth between our fingers as we pointed out little insects and got in touch and in tune with nature and all it shared with us, so much of which I had never before even stopped to see. The bright, intelligent, little beadlike eyes of a woolly caterpillar almost seemed to comprehend when I talked with him. A little butterfly lit on my wrist, and Dawn showed me how to make him my friend. He seemed to sense what we were saying and to feel our love. I remembered the many times I had chloroformed butterflies and stuck them on mats with pins. How deeply I apologized to their little relative for that torture, for sometimes the poor little creatures hadn't been completely dead when we had skewered them to the velvet. How bestial, almost like Hitler's unconcerned feelings for the Jews. I fell against a rotted tree trunk and saw myself for what I'd really been—a thoughtless, selfish specimen of nature unconnected with the feelings of the rest of life's circle. Even while it hurt to realize these things, I was glad I was beginning to see myself in relationship to the rest of the cosmos. As each thing was explained to me, I felt there was even more of my life that had to be changed. In fact there seemed to be very little that would not have to be restructured.

Through the rest of the day and all through the night we sat leaning against our little "tuled" sticks. Sometimes the pain of cramped muscles was excruciating; other times I wanted so much to sleep I literally thought I would die. I even tried to sleep with my eyes open so they wouldn't know, but there was always someone touching that nerve in my neck just as I began to lose contact with reality. Different speakers took over at different intervals until I wasn't sure what was real and what was a dream. Lack of sleep, physical discomfort, lack of food and water, new mind-blowing verbal concepts, and things I had read and seen in the past challenged my ability to reason.

For the biggest part of forty-eight hours we sat listening to new doctrines that sometimes seemed so exciting they made my blood curdle. Other times I found it hard to make sense out of the words. I wondered how long one could endure such physical and emotional stress. Was it really purifying us, conditioning us for higher things? Was it impossible to take other steps forward until after we had mastered this first, and some people felt, hardest one?

I wanted to know more. I longed to continue, but it became more and more difficult. A fly droned close to my ear and it seemed that it was talking instead of the speaker. I felt drugged, but I couldn't have been because I'd had nothing to eat or drink since arriving. At last, sweet peace began wrapping around me like a warm blanket. It enfolded everybody in the room in its softness. All of us were one! Just like Sky, who was speaking again, was saying: Oh how wonderful and comforting it was to be one with Jesus, to feel His great all-encompassing mind and know that as I progressed I would understand more about it and Him.

Time became confused. I remembered it was predawn when we'd first come, then one day had passed and one night, and another day and another night, and the sky was beginning to lighten again. All six neophytes who had come in with me had left. I felt proud that I was still able to remain, that they would let me, that I could take it.

From somewhere outside a trumpet called, and together we rose to our feet and were drawn towards it. It came from somewhere in the woods beyond where we had been before on our three little excursions.

"We're coming, Jesus. We're coming, Jesus. We're following in the paths You've trod. We're coming, Jesus, we're coming, Jesus. We're coming, precious Son of God," we sang over and over.

There was an air of expectancy around the little wooded area, and it wouldn't have surprised me at all if the trumpet really had been heralding the Second Coming.

Just as the sun shot out its first bright rays through the grayness, we rounded a corner and saw before us a shining lake about the size of a small swimming pool. Beside it stood two men in white, with their arms raised high above their heads. In the early morning breeze their soft robes ruffled gently like wings. It was so beautiful I found myself crying again, and weak with fatigue and hunger and awe, I was helped down the path by two members whose names I did not know. Birds were singing, crickets were chirping, and frogs were croaking. There could not have been a more beautiful place, a more beautiful sound, or a more beautiful feeling.

"Jesus loves you," the young man on my right whispered.

"I love Jesus," I replied.

"And I love you."

I stifled a sob, "I love you, and everybody and everything in the world more than I ever thought I could."

"You don't yet know how to really love."

I stumbled. I couldn't imagine it being any better than it was.

On the wild, dew-damp greenness we fell to the ground in prayer, and even though none of us had had any sleep for over sixty hours other than the catnaps we had had on the bus, sleep seemed the farthest thing from our minds. Sky told me again about my baptism, and behind a little screen I disrobed and put on the white garment that was handed to me. Then I was taken into the water and completely submerged while the two young men standing over me spoke a blessing in tongues. Sky gave me a new name, "Lilac." I loved it from the moment it fell out of his mouth. Lilacs had always been my favorite flowers since I had visited my uncle one spring and seen a whole hedge filled with them, white and pink and three different shades of purple. And the fragrance! Always after that occasion I had been able to close my eyes and remember it, even smell it. Now I would be a part of the fragrance and the beauty and the wonder forever.

After my baptism, Sky's voice was big and almost overwhelming while at the same time it was gentle and protecting. He looked directly at me and said, "Lilac, you are no longer Mary, she has vanished into your old world. From this moment on you have no connection with her or with the outside. You belong here in body and mind and soul. You are ours and we are yours, living here in harmony and love and peace, enlarging our capabilities every day in every way, getting closer to perfection in all things. We are one with Jesus."

Aloud I offered, "One with Jesus."

I was reborn, renamed, reenlightened, given new clothes—not really new, just new to me, and we all went back towards the house, singing, dancing, picking flowers, and placing them in each other's hair. I had never felt so elated, so loved, so at peace, so much as though I belonged, without reservation, just for myself, just the way I was, with all my faults and dumb little failings that I was sure, one by one, Sky and Trust and the others would help me overcome.

In the big room we were each given a mug of punch and a big chunk of homemade brown bread loaded with honey. When I first saw the tray of bread, I wondered for an instant if we would all charge at it like a bunch of starving dogs, since we hadn't eaten for so long, but we didn't. Each person waited patiently and politely for his or her name to be called to come and get his food. It was ambrosia! Never had bread tasted or smelled so good, and the drink . . . well, I was so grateful I could hardly get it down. I started crying again. I, who had hardly ever cried in the old world, had become the weepingest of babies, for everything was so overwhelming, so many new concepts. Actually, when I thought about it, the bread and punch were the first things I had ever truly been thankful for in my whole life. Always before, things had been given to me before I'd even asked. I had never been hungry in all my seventeen years upon earth, and just the thought of my never having given thanks to Jesus before for any of my blessings made me feel unworthy to eat now. What a wonderful lesson this had been. As for sleep, who was ever grateful or appreciative of that? Until now. Dawn led me to an upstairs dormitory and gave me a mat to roll out on. I think I fell asleep before I had even finished spreading it. Sleep . . . blessed, restful, usually unappreciated sleep. I dreamed in wild flamboyant colors and orchestrated sounds. Somewhere in the back of my mind I wondered if someone had put something in my drink, but of course they hadn't; I was just upped on life! It was as if always before I had seen it in black and white, in one dimension. Now I was seeing it in all its glory —flowers and rainbows and colors brighter than any of the big color boxes of ninety-seven crayons. I had a nightmare that it wasn't real and that I would wake up in my old mundane world of black and white, pain and pallor; I couldn't stand that! Oh no, dear Jesus, please, I couldn't stand that, not after I'd once been privileged to glimpse the glory of the eternities in Your brilliant colorful world.

It seemed as if I had only been asleep for minutes when I felt someone first touching and then grinding at that same sensitive nerve in my shoulder and neck.

The windows were open, and vaguely I could hear birds singing their little hearts out. A breeze ruffled through the curtains and brushed against my cheek like a soft hand. Someone was singing, "Jesus says it's time to work. In His Kingdom none must shirk." Gradually, the tempo picked up like a march. "Work, work, work, work, while we're here on earth. Heaven is the place for rest. We're working our way there. Work, work, work, work, while we're here on earth. Heaven is the place for rest, we're working our way there."

Gentle, a girl who had only been there two weeks, walked down the steps with me. It was strange. Again, I felt I had known her all my life. Usually I get all uptight and uncomfortable when I'm with someone I haven't known for a long time. To be perfectly honest, I'm usually uptight and uncomfortable with everybody, just to different degrees. But with her, a stranger, well, almost

31

a stranger I felt just as if she was an extension of myself. What a wonderful and satisfying and trusting new concept.

Gentle looked down at her wrist. "I really miss my watch. I know I won't need it here and shedding it and my jewelry along with my clothes and my old life-styles was, I guess, necessary." Her eyes misted. "But I . . . I . . . sure miss it."

I wondered about her parents, her background. There certainly was something back there she was missing terribly. I knew it wasn't her watch.

Dawn came between us. "Time for food and then work in the fields," she said softly. They didn't seem to like the new ones to be together too much.

I sided over with Gentle. She needed me. "Jesus loves you," I mouthed, then I added, "I love you too." It was nice to be needed.

The first few days at Haven House passed in a kind of blur. We worked from sunup till sundown, probably from 5:00 A.M. till 6:00 P.M., with only bread and the vegetables grown on the farm to eat. I knew it was a purifying process that would eventually end, but I had a nagging thread of fear running through me that I'd end before my time of probation.

It was funny how I missed meat and fruit and milk, mostly milk. I tried never to think about it, but the thoughts were always there, bugging little gnatlike distractions. At night we were so tired it seemed like it was 4:00 A.M., time to get up, before we'd hardly gotten to sleep.

At first it bothered me probably more than anything that I couldn't brush and floss my teeth; they seemed an inch thick in my mouth, but even that I adjusted to. I had had all my priorities so screwed up. Like Sky said, after we'd gotten our life-styles straightened out we could start doing what should be done in proper perspective. Like flossing teeth, I hoped.

One hot day Gentle pulled her long sleeves up and tucked them into her shoulder seams. I gasped when I saw the scarred needle tracks on her arms. She immediately sensed my reaction and pulled down the fabric. "I didn't want you to know," she faltered.

I tried to hide my shock, for the insides of both arms had been one bulging mass of scar tissue. "That was your other life."

A tear dripped out of one eye, "I hope so."

Almost without thinking I asked, "Is that the reason you're here?"

She nodded, "Nothing else could help me. My ever-so-good parents couldn't, psychiatrists couldn't, juvenile halls couldn't, foster homes couldn't". . . . her voice trailed off in defeat.

"Do you think Jesus can?" I asked, voicing the first doubt I had had.

She sniffed, "He's got to! He's my last hope."

I grinned, feeling more positive. "Jesus loves you."

"And I love Him."

I squeezed her arm, "And I love you."

She smiled back, "I trust you."

Her saying "trust" was even greater than her saying "love." Love was such an overused, abused word on the outs, meaning animal-like carnal sex, or deviation . . . or . . . I'd just have to concentrate on love in its true and undefiled connotation.

When it was time to eat, Gentle and I went over to a little clump of trees to evacuate. When she lifted up her long skirt, she showed me the back of her knees and even in her groin and in the roof of her mouth and her hairline where she had shot up until scar tissue and infection had built up big, almost rocklike, hard ridges. I wept, and wiping the tears away with my fingertips, I placed the salty moisture on the scars in her hairline.

"I know what Jesus meant now by compassion," I said softly.

She wiped her tears on the tips of her fingers and brushed them across my forehead. "And I'm beginning to understand what He meant by loving your neighbor as yourself."

I picked a little yellow flower and placed it in her hair. . . . "Don't ever, ever, ever forget that part about . . . *loving yourself.* That's one of the things I'm here to learn to do."

"Me too," she nodded, "Me too . . . maybe especially me!"

Someone called our names and we hurried over to eat and return to work.

I was happy when I saw that the blisters on top of blisters between my thumb and pointer finger had started to bleed again. It made me relate to some of the pain that Jesus, as well as my precious new sister Gentle, had suffered in her past. I felt guilty that I had had life so easy. Would I ever be really tested to the point of almost nonendurance as I was sure she had been, or would the worst of my Gethsemane be here where I had to go a few days without sleep and food and ache in my every joint because of physical labors my soft body was not used to?

I watched Gentle's pathetic little figure grubbing weeds up and down the long, never-ending rows with her little hand hoe. Dirt and sweat mixed together and ran in little crusted rivulets down her beautiful, childlike, innocent-looking face. Poor little sixteen-year-old baby. I was beginning to feel just a touch of what Jesus must feel. It was a good feeling even while it was a bad one. Oh, I hoped Gentle would make it this time! I'd pray and fast and do anything Sky asked in her behalf.

After the first three weeks of physical hell we

had the crops planted, and Sky said things would be easier for awhile. We'd have to weed and irrigate, but that apparently wasn't nearly so bad as preparing the twenty-four acres for planting.

I was really glad because Dawn had gotten so run down she was no longer able to work outside, and poor little Gentle was looking like a little wisp from one of those old paintings where the children are all eyes. I felt guilty when I thought about getting her on one of my mother's high protein diets with lots of wheat germ and fresh orange juice and cow's milk and . . . But things would get better. Sky had promised us that as soon as the crops were planted we'd take off a few days to rest and fast and pray for Dawn. I hoped he intended to include Gentle.

It was strange how after we'd worked all day until we thought we'd literally drop that we could come in and dance and sing and listen to lectures once we had our second wind.

I was learning to love Jesus more every day. How sad that parents would leave Jesus out of their children's lives.

I remembered how often the kids in my school had said they were searching for something to believe in, yearning for something to be dedicated to, to trust in, to feel secure with, to lead and guide them. I couldn't wait to go out to recruit new followers. I would be the greatest message carrier they ever had, or did everyone who went out feel that way? Did they all have the zeal of the apostles of old? This is what life is all about. It must be shared! My blood bubbled within me as I thought of doing it.

Between crop seasons Sky would have everyone dress as much like the outies as possible and drop off a load of them early in the morning at some nearby town. By nighttime, when he picked them up, they would always have more prospective followers than they could conveniently take back.

Sky had started his group only a few years before with two acres and three workers. Now he owned thirty acres including the little woods and the house and had a deposit on another house and a 200-acre farm farther upstate. That Haven could care for eventually up to 200 people, and each one of us would be part of that program. There we would have little children and a school and even facilities for higher learning. The possibilities were almost endless with Jesus's help. Sometimes I got so carried away I almost forgot about Him in the plan. That made me miserable, but Sky was patient. He had always said perfection wouldn't be easy.

I loved Sky. He had the most wonderful mind I had ever been around. Once he told me in confidence that at the university, where he got his BA in two and one-half years, they had told him he had an IQ of 170. That made me almost worship him, well, not really worship him, but certainly reverence him. Surely with that powerful mind and with the help of Jesus he knew what he was doing. I would never doubt him! That would be like doubting myself, which he said I must never do. Or doubting Jesus, which would be even worse!

Haven House was like an extended family, with all the aunts and uncles and cousins and brothers and sisters I'd never had. Brook told fortunes and read tea leaves and told me such wonderful things about my future that I could hardly stand it . . . how I would be instrumental in helping in a small way to make the world a better place in which to live, and how much love and good I would bring into the lives of others.

We'd sit around at night and sing and dance, and we'd make things with our hands and stretch our minds by talking and trying to grasp and understand all the mysteries of life and the great areas after life. It was stimulating, and I was content, even though a little part of me that I tried not to dwell on was always a bit tired and hungry. Sky said that was good for the soul. He knew so much about people and their actions and reactions. I knew he must have been a psychology major, but he would never tell me. He always said we must never allow our minds to think about the past. We should wipe it out as completely as we had wiped out the spirit world where we used to live before we came here to gain bodies and progress on to our next world.

One night Dawn died. We anointed her with oil and perfume we had made from flowers. Then, after wrapping what was left of her frail little body in our finest white linen, we laid it in the back of the van so Trust and Sky could take it to its final resting place.

Then we had a feast and celebrated her progress to a Haven beyond ours. Sky lectured about how happy and how whole and blessed she was in her new state and how we should glory with her. At first it wasn't easy for me because, like everyone else, I had been conditioned to think of death as sad; but soon Sky even had me singing "Hosanna" for the great thing that had happened to her.

It's strange how sincere and yet how off people can be on the outs. I remember my Great-grandma's funeral. People cried and mourned and acted as if it was the worst thing in life. Here we were treating it like a special occasion. Happy for Dawn, singing and dancing, and praising that she was now with Jesus, actually and literally and forever in His glorious kind and loving presence.

"Jesus loves you, too," I kept saying over and

over to everyone around me. It sounded dumb and nondescriptive of what I really wanted to convey, but there are no words to express some emotions and feelings.

I saw Gentle sitting alone. "What's the matter?" I asked.

"I dunno."

"You look sad."

"Yeah."

"Don't you understand about Dawn?"

"Yeah."

"Aren't you happy for her?"

"Yeah."

"Now, I don't understand."

Gentle moaned and curled up in my arms like a little child. "It's me . . . I . . . I want to . . . to . . . to be with Dawn."

I didn't comprehend.

"Why couldn't it have been me who died? I'm no good to nobody, not even myself. I'm not helping you guys here, I'm sickly and weak and a poop-out . . . I . . . ."

"Jesus loves you just as you are." It was the most compelling thing I could say.

"How can He love me when I hate myself?" Between mangled sobs, words slipped between her lips. "I want a fix so bad you'll never know! I live from one hour to the next wondering if I'll make it. Sometimes sure I will, sometimes sure I won't. Often I feel I love drugs more than I love Jesus."

I held her so tight she gasped.

"Oh, Lilac, what am I ever, ever, ever going to do?"

I shook my head. The readjustment into my new life had been so relatively easy for me, though more often than I cared to think about, little shadows of my parents swept across the corners of my mind. But I knew they were better off without me, so I turned my head and brushed them away. With poor Gentle, of course I couldn't understand. I'd never been there. Drugs and booze had never held that much fascination for me. I didn't want anything that blurred my thinking or interfered with my controlling my own destiny. I had always gotten real paranoid when I'd used. It wasn't worth it. Gentle was different. Her needs and controls were different. Maybe we could have a few days of fast for her. I promised her I'd talk to Sky about it.

That night Gentle cut her wrists. It was the only way she felt she could be sure of getting into the Kingdom. Her scrawled little note was pathetic. She knew Dawn would be lonely and would help her adjust. Her last line I couldn't get out of my mind: "Oh, dear Jesus, please don't let there be any dope in Heaven."

We had the same celebration for her as we'd

had for Dawn, but somehow I couldn't rejoice. Dawn had been older—maybe twenty-five. Little Gentle was barely getting started in her life.

I asked Sky if he was going to inform her family.

"What family?" he asked, "We are her family!" His eyes looked through me. "For a girl as intelligent as you are, sometimes I'm not sure you're worthy." I felt as if I had been kicked out of the realms of Heaven into the darkness of Hell. After all Sky had taught me and done for me, how could I have ever questioned him?

My sorrow debilitated me, and Trust, sensing my despair, suggested I do penitence for a few days by only eating bread instead of the regular diet of mush in the morning, and carrots, potatoes, onions, and cabbage for the day's other meal. I offered to fast, but he said I needed my energy to keep up my divine duties.

When my three-day fast of bread and water was over, I found a divine book on my bed. I knew it was from Sky and that I had been forgiven. I could hardly stand the wonder of it.

I think my penance made me even closer to Sky. He held the Priesthood of the Deities, and I had forgotten it. Maybe my background with a Mother who was for ERA had made it even more difficult for me to appreciate the man's role in the scheme of life. I would never forget again.

When our new crops came in, Sky was elated. There had been frosts around the area that had wiped out most of the other fields, but ours in a protected little valley had survived. He would easily make enough to get the new project going and maybe even make a down payment on a third Haven. It was glorious. The cause was growing. It really is true that if you keep the Commandments you will prosper.

On my first trip out as a fund raiser I was scared. What if people would reject me, what if I couldn't explain to them the message of love and protection and trust and freedom from fear and pressure? I wished that I had Dawn or Gentle to go with. They had both been so special. I still missed them even though it made me feel guilty. No one was supposed to even think of them. Their names and everything had gone on to the other world. Our thoughts could pull them down towards this one, hurting them, handicapping them. I certainly didn't want to do that.

Trust said I was to work with Hope, and I wished I didn't have to. She was one of the older ones, and . . . I don't know . . . we were just different. Besides, fund raising made me feel I was begging . . . or worse still, that I wasn't quite honest. Trust had lectured and lectured to make us understand that carnal people wouldn't give for divine purposes; so we would have to say that we were raising money to keep needy children in camps for the summer, or that we were raising money for a lost-animal shelter. I hated it, but I guess you have to do anything any way you can for the right cause.

I found a girl about my age literally screaming out in a nonvocal way that she was dying for someone to help her, to care for her, to show her a pathway out of loneliness and despair and misery. I was so tuned in to her silent scream that it hurt my insides with its intensity. "Jesus loves you," I said softly.

She didn't answer. "No backbone, no spine, no pride," my Mom used to say to me when I had the downs. I could hear Mom's voice echoing from my past world, "Stand up like you've got some spunk, like you know who you are and where you're going!"

This girl was well dressed. She looked intelligent, but she was unhappy, unfulfilled, depressed. She walked the way she felt.

I stayed a few steps behind her. It took a long time for me to get up enough courage to say, "Jesus really does love you, did you know that?"

We had been carefully tutored on how to touch other people, but now I was trying too hard, wanting too desperately to not lose one soul. I was pushing too much, going too fast, but I couldn't help myself. Everything was spilling out before she asked for it, and that was not the way at all.

I bit my lip until I could feel the taste of blood. An important contact and I was muffing it. What would Sky say? Would I be ostracized again? I couldn't stand that!

The tears were welling up in my eyes. I had to go somewhere where I could hide them, and myself. As I turned like a hurt dog to find a place where I could be alone with my sorrow and failure, I felt rather than saw that the girl had turned and was now following me.

"How do you know Jesus, or anybody else for that matter, loves me?" she asked in a tense voice.

"Oh, I know He loves you," I said with the deepest of conviction. I wished I could put my feelings into words but I couldn't. Everything seemed so light and superficial and garbled, but apparently she felt my inner message because together we walked to a bench and sat down.

She listened to my message and related to me, but her needs weren't quite severe enough for her to change to another life-style. She had a boyfriend with whom she'd had a quarrel because her parents, particularly her Mother, weren't happy that they were spending weekends together in his apartment while his other roommates were still there. Something about the whole setup made her feel her parents weren't really so concerned about her virtue as about what people would say and how the setup would look to *their* friends.

After awhile I could see that, even though the girl was hurting, she wasn't ready for a higher life-style. She was too imprisoned by the physical. But at least she was into astro projection and transcendental meditation, and sometimes those are the first steps. Anyway, she gave me eight dollars.

Sky had told us it would be fairly easy to get money, but that we might have to contact ten or twenty, or even thirty or forty or 1,000 people before we would find one ready to accept our great truths and then live them. It was hard to be that patient and long-suffering and persevering. The time was so close. Everything was so imperative. I wanted to give up, but I made myself think as Sky had told us to of Jesus walking through the barren hills around Bethany and Nazareth and along the lush green meadows around the Sea of Galilee, trying to get people to listen to His message. How much less prepared and capable I was than He, but I still had been called to proclaim His gospel, and I would. I would share it as I would the most wonderful thing in my life. I sat down on the curb, smiling, remembering the time when I had been in third grade and Ginny, my little girlfriend, had run over with a new kind of ice cream from 31 Flavors. Together we had sat on our lawn. We had a house then with a yard and a flower bed and even a few little rows of radishes and carrots and strawberries. Ginny and I had gurgled and smacked and "Ummmmmmmmmed" with delight, as we had taken turns licking drips off the side of the cone.

I hadn't been able to wait to run in and share with my parents this wonderful new taste I had found, nor could I wait to tell my other friends. It had just been too wonderful, too special, too yummy to keep to myself. I felt the very same way a hundred times over about Sky's Jesus Movement. I wanted to share it with the whole world. It was too good not to! I wanted to stand up on the curb and start screaming about what all the people who were passing me by were missing. But Sky had said that was not the way, that a one-to-one contact was what he wanted, what Jesus wanted. It had to be right.

I hated myself when a couple of cute dudes in a Corvette drove by, and instead of trying to pick me up, asked me the way to the nearest haystack. I wanted to flip them the bird, but I resisted and then felt deadly ashamed that I had even had the urge. I had a long way to go before I'd even get out of the First Kingdom. Would I ever make it up to the Third, where Sky was, or ever, ever, up to the Fourth where Jesus dwelt?

I contacted gobs of kids and even one older lady walking down the street with an armload of groceries, but I couldn't turn any of them on to the message. Were they dense? Candidates for a lower kingdom? Was I a failure? It would almost be worse letting Sky down than letting myself down. He expected so much of us and had such love and confidence in me. I *couldn't* let him down! I'd be more careful about casing prospects. I'd be more humble and prayerful, be more tuned in to their vibrations, leave more up to Jesus Himself. I deserved His help; I'd been fasting since the day before. I could tell from where the sun sat in the sky that in only an hour or so it would be time for the minibus to pick us up and I'd only raised $37.45. Would I dare go to the bus? Sky said we should aim for at least $100 each. The humiliation of it, the shame. But maybe that's what I needed —humbling, for on any number of occasions during the day I had felt quick shots of envy as I looked at some girl's expensive leather jacket or saddleback pants. Or as some of the neat sports cars had passed by, or as some jock in his tight pants had, against my will, caught my eye. Maybe I wasn't worthy of being in the Haven at all, but oh I needed it so. I needed it now probably more than I ever had. I was a foreigner in this land of physical degeneracy and wild uncontrolled passions, of dishonesty and dishonor, of hostility, rape, killing, and robbery. I wanted to go back to the protection and security of even my lower First

Kingdom; how much better it was than this. But would they, could they accept me back with my measly little $37.45? What would I do if they didn't? I became desperate, and there were very few people left around on the streets to contact.

Wearily, I started towards the place where I would be picked up, trying to figure out how I could convince Sky that I needed another chance, that I could, I really could, be a help in the cause of righteousness. Before our next fund raising and message carrying effort I would fast for three days before, as some of the others had done this time. Three days with only small amounts of water. I could do that. I hated myself for not having been strong enough to have done it this time. One day of fasting just wasn't enough to get into the spirit.

On the bus I felt better. It had been a hard day for everybody. Ten message carriers had gone out, and only two new followers had been brought back. But even two souls brought into the Kingdom were precious in His sight and a cause for rejoicing. We all started singing, "Jesus loves you, this is true, and He wants to help you too. Lift your arms and heed His call. He is calling, calling all. Say you love Jesus. Say you love Jesus. Say you love Jesus and feel the joy that brings."

As we sang the simple little song over and over again, waving our arms over our heads like hosanna branches, I would feel the same joy building inside me that I had felt when I climbed on the bus for the first time. It reverberated again from the back to the front, encompassing and comforting and lifting everyone on board. My mind and my body became part of it. I was not weak or weary or hungry any more. I was part of the wonder and gloriousness of it. We were all one, one with the music and the words and the love. Our hearts and our souls and our minds entwined.

It was so safe being back with others like myself where I wouldn't have to be tempted by worldly things. At a high school I'd passed, I had not even been brave enough to face the fact that I had been almost irresistibly drawn inside. I loved learning. I yearned for it. I needed it. But Sky said that must wait until we had first built up the physical kingdom. We were like the Jews who had gone back to Israel and lived in communes, working, slaving, drudging, not having time for mental things in the beginning while they were laying down the physical foundation. No great edifice could be built without first putting forth the sweat and energy and know-how to structure a strong and everlasting base. Then would come the mental things in all their glory. Even more glorious because of the sacrifice that had gone before.

I had missed my parents, too, in my short excursion into the old world. Once a gray Mark IV like my Mom's had passed, and I had wanted to run out and stop it. Maybe it had been her. She wouldn't have recognized me, but I . . . I . . . sometimes it wasn't that easy to shut her out. I'd have to try harder. "One could not go forward if one lived in the past," Sky said.

I was glad they were singing the "I am thankful for . . ." song. It made me think about the happy things instead of the sad, the grateful things instead of the bad, and I needed that.

Moss had been one of the few who had brought in a new follower, a big fat girl with greasy, stringy hair and pimples like erupting volcanoes on her face. A moment of hostility grabbed me, and I could see her pulling the huge watering wagon, straining and sweating while I stood behind her with a whip. I quickly said a little prayer of repentance and wondered if it was she or myself I was angry at, or maybe even Moss because she had brought someone into the fold and I had not. Should I tell Sky about my weak, evil thought, or should I just do penance by myself? I'd do that! I'd fast for another half day. I couldn't make it much longer because I'd get too weak, and there was always so much work to do. Sky had found an outlet that would take all the tole painting and macrame hangers we could make and all the pots and jars we could throw on the new potter's wheel he had bought.

At first we had been restoring the house in our spare time, but that would have to wait. Enlarging the Kingdom would have to come first. The Second Coming was so close! So very frighteningly close! Sky was talking about building a plastic covered greenhouse so we could grow hanging basket plants, but either we'd have to get a lot of new devotees, or we'd have to wait until after our current crop was sold. There just were not enough hours in the day for one more project as things stood.

Sky's face clouded as he saw that we had brought in only two new members. I was glad that I had come when I had because now they had only a very simple short indoctrination and fellowshipping period, only one day and one night of fasting and lectures; then we were back in the fields. It was sad in a way because they needed that spiritual welding.

After only two days Wanda, the big fat girl Moss had brought in, disappeared during the night. She'd never really been one with us; she was too lazy and undedicated and searching. Sky must have known from the beginning that she wouldn't stay because even the new name he had given her hadn't quite fit into our culture. The other new one belonged from the beginning. Sky renamed him Maize and the way he worked was an inspiration to us all. Maize had grown up on a farm in the Mideast. His Father had been a brutal man who whipped the kids with a horsewhip for the least infraction and bullied them and belittled their physical ability. At the Haven, Maize was treated as he always should have been, as someone big and special in his own way. Not too bright, but strong enough to do the work it would take three of us girls to do. He was like a big, happy, tail-wagging puppy dog to have around, and our appreciation of his strength made him blossom like a green growing thing.

He had run away from home when he was fourteen and had been a street kid for four years, doping, stealing, whatever had to be done to exist, but never liking himself for doing those things he always had felt were wrong. Now he was in his natural element, appreciated for what he was and what he could do, accepted and loved without reservations. It was hard on him though to exist on as little food as we were allotted. Sky felt gorging was a sin, so most of us ate sparingly and stopped while we were still hungry. With Maize I often saw his eyes drop to the floor as the second helping of bread came by; none of us took it though we all wanted to. It was part of our personal and physical disciplining as well as for our spiritual health.

Once I saw Maize, after his little trip to relieve

his bladder, pick up a handful of some kind of growing stuff and eat it. He wouldn't touch any of the things we were growing to market, but he would eat grass or whatever, like a cow or something. It made me sad. Maybe he was giving up more than any of the rest of us, but surely he would be blessed for it. I said an extra little prayer for him that night. He was the big, gentle, teddy bear brother I would never have, and I knew he would protect me with his life if that were ever necessary. It was a nice comforting feeling. One couldn't have too many friends, too much family, too many people who loved them.

Sky believed in celibacy, and that was all right with most of us who never seemed to have enough energy or time to do what had to be done anyway, or at least what was expected of us or we expected of ourselves. Sometimes I tried to analyze how Sky always was able to make his ideas seem like our ideas, but I couldn't. Anyway it didn't really matter. We were doing what was best for us in our eternal progression and for Jesus and our fellowmen also. That was the important thing!

One night I woke up worrying about Wanda, the big-mouthed fat girl who'd left us. What if she went to the police and reported any of the things that the outs wouldn't understand? I could hardly wait for morning.

I missed breakfast so I could catch Sky. "You

look worried," he said. He was fantastic about nonverbal communication.

I felt embarrassed. He sensed everything. Would mentioning Wanda seem like I mistrusted his ability?

He looked me straight in the eye and patted my head like a child, "You know I love you, Lilac. I trust you. I know you wouldn't hurt me any more than I'd hurt you."

I kind of stuttered, "Oh . . . it's nothing."

He hugged me, "Honestly, Lilac, I know you meant only to help me."

"It's . . ."

"It's what?"

I didn't want to tell him but I had to. "What if Wanda, I mean Jade . . . would hurt you . . . I mean . . . like go. . . ."

Sky's voice vibrated with emotion, "Precious blessed Lilac—now you are becoming all the things Jesus and I want you to be. More concerned with others' welfare than your own. More concerned about eternal things than now things. More concerned about my safety and well-being than . . ." He led me over to a quiet corner, "Never forget who I am, Lilac," his voice lowered, ". . . or my connection through Jesus for you." He seemed to be listening, then he smiled, "Jesus loves and appreciates what you've done, too."

My heart raced.

Our other crops started coming in more bountifully than we had ever hoped. Sky and Maize and Trust took all our trucks and vans full to the wholesale market every day. It completely changed our schedules. We often had to finish picking and packing by flashlight so that we could get things loaded. Our produce had to be at the wholesale market around 2:00 A.M.

Each day it seemed as if we had less and less sleep, for with irrigating, and weeding, picking and packing, there simply were not enough hours. But somehow it was really satisfying. We were part of creating and building a new cosmos. I'm sure all the others felt as I did—we were almost like pioneers with a whole new concept in living, from which would shoot all the worthwhile attributes of the good and wholesome life with Christ at the head and Sky just under Him.

It was worth working our tails off for. In our Second Kingdom we would be above physical things and into the mental—then we could rest.

In our Third Kingdom we would be above mental things and into spiritual. That I could not comprehend at all, but it was merely because I had not progressed to the point where I could.

Truth was truth. Just because I could not understand, that made only me, not it, implausible. Oh what a glorious day it would be when I progressed to that Third Kingdom, or even to the Second.

Occasionally, when I was so exhausted physically, mentally, and emotionally that I could hardly manage one foot in front of the other, I wondered if I would ever make it, or if anyone would, except Sky.

When fall came, we all celebrated. Painting tole trays and making macrame fishbowl and flowerpot holders would seem like a vacation. And going out to get new followers for the big new Haven would be exciting. We'd really have to get some divine help in that undertaking because Sky eventually wanted 200 there. We would have to build long dormitories and a huge kitchen; the house would be used mainly for projects like the tole and macrame work.

Sky strongly denounced groups that used drugs and participated in sex and didn't work. "Idleness is the devil's workshop, and we'll see that he never comes here."

I rubbed my aching neck and right arm. "If the devil dared come here, even he'd be put to work," I thought.

Sky didn't seem to be able to do anything wrong. A land developer came by and offered him three quarters of a million dollars for Haven House. After dickering a little bit, he eagerly accepted it. I had heard the whole negotiation because I had been out cleaning the well when the men drove up. At first I had just squatted down behind it to hide; then I'd stayed there because I was too embarrassed to leave. Dealing in money matters was of all carnal things the most carnal for everyone but Sky, and he only did it so we could exist in the Tainted Kingdom.

Within a week he'd bought a big truck and an enormous trailer and moved us all to Haven Two. It had much more usable land, most of which would be worked by machinery. But I missed the little woods and especially the tiny lake where we had planned to farm trout. That was to have been my project. But I guessed I shouldn't be selfish enough to stand in the way of progress, and maybe later on we'd be able to dig our own little lake down where the water drained out of the lower field.

Sky desperately needed people to make Haven Two go and three days after we arrived there he sent us out as message carriers. Jesus would provide, he told us, and we went out fasting and knowing He would if we'd keep our hearts open and allow Him to influence our approach to people.

Outside the bus station the first day I met a gentle young girl who was as hopelessly lost as anyone I'd ever seen. Her Mother was an alcoholic, and her real Father had abused her from the time she was seven. We were like two magnets being drawn together, and my sharing the program with her made me feel the way I had felt back in the third grade when I first shared my newfound flavor of "best in the world" ice cream with my friends.

Three days later we went out, and I found another contact behind the local high school, a girl who had already tried to commit suicide five times. Jesus would not only save her life, He'd save her soul.

It was funny about Jody. By looking at her and watching her life-style you'd think she had everything anybody would want out of life, but those were only exterior things. Inside she was a rotting mass of confusion, insecurity, and frustration. On the outside she overcompensated by being loud and aggressive, but that was just to cover all the other deeper, more important needs that were not being fulfilled.

I related to her immediately and knew in the Kingdom we would become the closest of sisters. I would help her learn all the concepts and important forever dimensions I had added to my life.

It was amazing how I had changed and grown in . . . could it possibly be just a little over six months? But my mind had been spiritually opened, and with Sky instructing us for fifteen minutes each morning at breakfast, and twenty minutes each noon while we ate dinner, and one hour each night, my whole body as well as my spirit was being submerged in the wonder of his concepts, Jesus's concepts, eternal concepts.

In Kingdom Two we were beginning to be fed doctrine so deep I could hardly stand the wonder of it. Sky was really the Elijah who would come to be the forerunner of Jesus the Christ just before His Second Coming, just as John the Baptist had been the forerunner before His first appearance. My heart always skipped a few beats when I thought of Sky literally talking with Jesus, planning for Him and with Him about His very-soon-to-be second sojourn on earth. My eyes always misted with tears when I considered that we . . . that I—would be called "assistant," just down a step from Sky in Jesus's great new theocratical government that would be set up. I would be all the things my Mother always wanted me to be: a queen and a ruler, but not with any self-aggrandizement—just awe and glory and the joy of serving. I must sacrifice even more of my time and energies. I must fast even oftener for more humbleness and awareness. I must work even harder!

The depths to which I would fall if I ever slipped from my now attained station were so great and terrible that I tried, as Sky urged us, never to think about them: eternal Hell with Satan and his worshipers, never to be forgiven in this world or in any of the worlds to come; fire and brimstone, hate and strife, or contention and discord and loneliness because no one person cared about another. That was the part of Hell we now had upon the earth and could understand and relate to—the selfishness, the hurtings of one person to another, whether physical, mental, or psychological; the loneliness, the depression, the anger, and the pain. Oh, I didn't want that; no one in his right mind should want that for eternity, yet that was the direction in which most people were going, those unwilling to sacrifice a little during this short period of life's testing for the great and glorious eternal future that awaited us all if we lived to be deserving of it.

I wanted to go out and throw my arms around everyone in the outside world, tell them how much Jesus loved them, how much we loved them, and invite them into the fold. But like Sky said, "Most of them had been blinded by the craftiness of men and by the cunning ways of Satan and already, knowingly or unknowingly, they had bound their lives with his, sold their birthrights, their bodies, and their eternal lives."

I wanted to weep for them, but Sky said energies and time were too precious to waste now that the great and glorious event was so very, very close. I wondered if Jesus was actually going to start His reign here on earth next week, next month, next year, . . . or tomorrow! Sky wouldn't

tell us and he was the only one other than Jesus
and God themselves who knew. Even the angels
in the Fourth and Fifth Heavens, the Bible said,
had not been informed.

On October 4, when all the others were asleep,
Sky called me into his Holy of Holies. I was more
afraid than I had ever been in my life. What if I
had inadvertently done something to make me
unworthy of further progression? The pain and
guilt was so severe I could hardly walk. Every
negative thing I had ever said or done expanded
in my mind like great black balloons. Outside his
holy door he opened the four great keyed bolts
that hung one above the other and were always
locked. Nobody was allowed inside the Holy of
Holies except Sky. It was there that he discussed
plans with Jesus for the sanctification of the new,
peaceful, bright, love-filled earth that would exist
after Jesus came to take over. But first the wicked
would be burned as a stubble. Is that what Sky was
going to tell me, that I, because of all my weaknesses and insecurities, would be one of those
burned, cast out into eternal darkness with weeping and wailing and gnashing of teeth? Being shut
out of the Kingdom could only mean that.

Inside the Holy of Holies, bright fluorescent
lights made everything in the small room almost
give off its own glow, or was the light coming
from Sky or some other source? I dared not think

about it. Sky sat me down on a little stool in the center of the small room and looked deep into my eyes, past the cornea and the fluid into my brain.

"Lilac, my child, you have been a good and trusted servant in the Kingdom," he said quietly.

I could only weep.

"You have made yourself worthy of higher blessings."

I sobbed quietly.

"You are ready for the first step into Kingdom Three."

A heavy tremor shook my body. The Third Kingdom where Jesus came? "No, no," I said softly, "I am unworthy."

Sky clasped both my hands in his, "Your humility and dedicated strivings make you worthy." He paused, "You are ready for your Sacred and Third Kingdom name."

I couldn't stop the shaking of my body. Somewhere I had read that ancient Indian tribes give their chosen people sacred names by which they shall be known in the worlds beyond. Was this part of the great secret of this Universe, plus all the other worlds that the great God had created? I bowed my head. Tears streamed down my face and puddled in my lap. Sky put his hands upon my head and gave me a blessing so beautiful I could hardly bear the joy of it. Then he gave me the new name, the one by which I would be called when this world was perfected, the name by which only Sky and the angels and Jesus Himself should call me on this earth.

I could not bear the strain and fainted. When I woke up, Sky was tucking me in on a mat in the big main room. I found it hard to believe reality was just that. It was too glorious! I? I? How could they ever have chosen me. Now I would have to try even harder. I wondered how many days I could fast in complete thanksgiving and still do justice to the work that was expected of me. How many others of the group had had the same sacred, overwhelming eternal experience? No one would ever know for I had been sworn to secrecy on my very life and with the threat of being given to Satan if I should ever divulge what I had heard and seen and been promised, to dwell ever as the lowest servant in his kingdom. But I would never, never, never do that! I would give my life before I would break the sacred oaths and covenants I had made during my consecration and dedication.

Shortly after my blessed experiences in the Third Kingdom, I caught cold. My throat hurt until I could hardly get our rough food down it, and my chest was squeezed as with some giant invisible hand. I tried to keep up with my work because Sky needed me, Jesus needed me, the program needed me. But each day I felt worse and weaker. I was glad when I was chosen to go out message carrying. Sky desperately needed more hands in the fields and in the different projects that he kept adding one to another. We were all so busy we never had time to think about our own problems and needs, and Sky had become more selective about the people he accepted into the group. These were the very last of the last days, he said, and there was no time to rehabilitate. We should bring in only the people who were eagerly and anxiously willing to be engaged in the final work and who would be dedicated to personal hardship and privation for the cause of a glorious and eternal future.

In a way it made it almost easier to spread the word, as that seemed to be what people were looking for, something to be dedicated to. We even began to bring in a few retired people, men and women who were still healthy enough to work hard and were looking for something to believe in, to live and sweat and toil for. The end was so close that we were all becoming almost desperate in our zeal. And it paid off. Never did we go back without the minibus being loaded till the tires were almost flat.

On one trip to a fairly small town I saw a man about the age of my Father have a heart attack as he was trying to get into his car. I hurried over to him and placed my hands on his head and prayed for him in one continuous round as he was waiting for the ambulance. Apparently the crowd that gathered thought I was his daughter and no one asked me to leave. I could tell from the look on the man's face that even in his great pain I was giving him peace. And when at one time someone tried to pry me away to give him air, the look in his eyes told them he needed me. When his spirit left his body just seconds before the ambulance got there, I knew that he had accepted Jesus, that his love and mine had joined together in the forever binding. "Hosanna, Hosanna, blessed be your peace and joy in Jesus," I said softly as they were loading his body on the stretcher. Then I began to chant the happy song about the joy of death. It made me sad that no one in the crowd understood. They looked at me almost with disgust that I should think this a happy occasion, poor lost, lonely souls who would be burned at Jesus's coming.

I informed Sky about the man's death, and he told me to forget it. I should have been out saving those who could come to the Kingdom and work out their own salvation. But I couldn't stop thinking about the man. He reminded me more and more of my own Stepfather, maybe wrong, maybe disillusioned, maybe of the world but still . . . some part of me still called to him and my Mom.

My next time in a town I borrowed an envelope and paper from a girl and sat down under a tree by the courthouse and wrote a long letter to my folks, telling them how much I loved them, and how I wished they too, could be reunited with me in the Kingdom. I told them how physically I was not well, but that spiritually I was progressing with greater rapidity than I had ever thought possible. In fact my gradually growing illnesses only seemed to be intensifying my spiritual growth. I pleaded with Mom and Frank to listen to the truths of the Jesus people if they ever came across them, that perhaps one day we might meet again in this life as well as being together in the coming worlds. Then I closed the letter with all the personal little scratches, crosses, and hearts and flowers I had used when I wrote them notes as a child. With tears I sealed the envelope and went to the post office to beg a stamp from somebody. How my parents would suffer to see me there begging, but they were the ones confused, not me. Oh, how I wished I could go home and straighten them out, but that would be impossible. I must put them out of my mind as I had all the other worldly things. But it was hard. I wanted my Mom to load me down with vitamin C and make me hot milk and honey and lemon and her own special made-from-scratch chicken soup.

I fainted again on the post office steps but got put together before anyone could cart me away to a hospital or a doctor. I had begun to faint more often, but maybe I was fasting too much, or it was just my rotten cold that I couldn't seem to get rid of, or something. Man, I really did feel awful and I had gotten so thin that even my underwear wouldn't stay up.

I considered telling Sky how awful I felt, but surely if it were anything serious he'd know, and he had enough things on his mind with all the expansions and everything without having to be bothered with my minor little aches and pains. The end of time was so close at hand there weren't even seconds to spare for anything outside of the almost frantic preparations for that great day and the glories that would come after it.

At first I thought I was having a nightmare. Two huge men had literally grabbed me out of the field and forced me into their car. Sky and all the group were running towards us, but in a crashing of gears and a cloud of dust we were bumping and banging over the winding, pock-filled dirt road leading toward the highway. Why would these men want me? Were they sadists? It couldn't be a kidnapping!

"Why? Why me?" I asked in a trembling voice.

Neither one of the men answered.

I sat shivering between them, thinking the most awful things it was possible for a human mind to conceive. I knew I would be willing to die for

Jesus and our cause in a dignified manner, but
. . . the deprogramming we'd been told about
. . . torture . . . indignation . . . degradation. I
wondered how much I could stand. What if they
tried to get me to tell the eternal secrets. Oh, I
couldn't tell, I wouldn't even with the most de-
praved kind of torturing. Or would I? I felt so
weak and sickly. Oh, dear Jesus, help me bear
anything that had to be borne. I could, I could
with His help. I had made it through months of
self-discipline and preparation. Sky had said he
had prepared us for the time when someone sa-
tanic would try to break us down. Even our Fa-
thers and Mothers might be Satan's tools. Could
that be it? Could my letter have . . .?

Quietly I asked, "Did my Mom and Frank send
you?"

Both men ignored me. They were now on the
highway speeding to who knew where. I couldn't
stand it. I simply couldn't stand the strain and I
began to heave and cough. I couldn't breathe. My
chest hurt as if someone was chopping at it with
an ax. After awhile both men became alarmed and
tried to comfort me. They stopped at a drive-in,
and parking some distance away, the driver said
he'd go in and get me some orange juice; the
other man suggested he get me a hamburger and
some fries and an extra thick malt. "The poor kid
looks like just a skeleton of her picture."

That made me relax some. They had to have gotten the picture from my folks who might, as Sky said, have become tools of Satan. Still I knew they'd never knowingly hurt me and I'd soon convince them about the wonder of Sky's program and be back in his tender eternal charge.

Somewhere in the back of my mind I remembered that it was almost time for my eighteenth birthday, as the outside world calculated things. In the Kingdom we measured from our baptism and rebirth. But here I would be eighteen . . . well, sometime soon. Was that the reason I had been kidnapped? Did they have to do it while I was still a minor? I tried to ask, but the man at the wheel again ignored me. Now that my uncontrolled hacking cough had stopped, he had regained his cool.

When the food came, I tried to decide what Sky would have me do. I knew it gave one strength to fast, but maybe in this case going into a wordly situation I needed worldly nourishment.

I felt more than guilty as the sweet thick malt slipped down my throat. I hadn't had any milk since I'd left home . . . and the hamburger, I fought myself to keep from snarfing it like a dog.

We drove for about three hours, then stopped in front of a nondescript little office building. I noticed first thing that it was Monterey-type with fancy ornamental wrought-iron grilles over the windows. Disguised bars, but bars nonetheless. I began to be scared silly again.

A smiling, don't-you-dare-touch-me type young woman led us to a little back room. It was very noncommital. After the first "How are you today?" and all that superficial, "I don't really care" outside world nothingness, everything was written down on long sheets of paper. Then everybody left and I was alone . . . really, really alone. It was almost as though Jesus, too, had left me. Quiet sobs began to wrack my body, noiseless dry upheavals that crushed and mangled my insides. I was tired—so heavily drugged tired that I could hardly keep my head upright. It was as though my neck had turned to overcooked spaghetti.

I could hear someone talking outside the door. It opened, and a middle-sized, brown-haired, brown-faced, brown-suited man entered.

"Hi, I'm Dave," he said, not too lightly, not too seriously.

I didn't reply.

"How are things going, Mary?"

I still didn't answer. For one second there I'd almost forgotten that Mary was the old outside me.

"I'm going to help you."

My voice came back, "I don't need any help."

"But surely you know you're sick," he said kindly.

I nodded, "I've got a little cold."

His face looked tense. "Sure, sure."

"I wanna get out of here," I gasped.

"Yeah, I know," he said with a deep sigh.

I'm not really sure about what happened after that, but when I came to I was in a doctor's office propped on his examination table. He was putting something that smelled rotten, and made me feel like he was pouring red hot coals inside my chest, up to my nose. Granola! What a time I'd picked to faint. I'd at least been picking better places than that in the past.

"I think you've got pneumonia, young lady," the doctor said kindly. Or was he just in on the conspiracy to keep me away from my Kingdom?

"Whatever is wrong with me will heal with faith and prayer," I said, trying to bolster up my own strength.

He shook his head gravely the way Doctor Marcus Welby used to do on TV. "Sometimes it does," he said grimly, "but most of the time it doesn't, so we're not going to take any chances. We'll just give you some antibiotics."

"You can't do that without my permission," I tried to protest.

"But he can with mine," Dave interrupted,

"I've been given power of attorney over you."

"What a pain in the ass you are," I said, feeling compelled in some way to take out my hostility.

"You'll probably say worse things than that about me," he said with resignation, "before we get through with each other."

"What do you mean?" I demanded. But he had left the room, and the doctor's nurse was preparing me for an examination. She put me on a scale with only a sheet around me, "Five foot five and one half inches and only eighty-nine pounds!" she said.

I couldn't believe it. I knew I'd lost weight, but eighty-nine pounds! The doctor checked my eyes and mouth: "Slight jaundice, malnutrition, teeth in terrible condition . . . probable pneumonia," plus a lot of technical stuff I didn't understand. So . . . maybe I'd stay just long enough to get put together physically and then go back. I was sooooooooooooo tired.

For three days I stayed in some dinky little hospital. Dave came in every day and tried to talk, but I wouldn't cooperate. Once I told him I wanted to see my folks. I was sure I could convince them I should go back to Sky, but he said no one could see me except him and the doctor till I'd got my act together. I began taking all my hate and frustration out on him. He really was a tool of Satan, but Sky had told me I would meet

73

people like that and he'd made me strong. I could withstand them all in the outside world. I would get back to Sky and the Kingdom. Someday someone would make a mistake and leave me alone with a door unlocked or something. With Jesus by my side I couldn't fail, and there was so very, very much work still to do to prepare for His glorious coming. I wanted to be a part of it! I had to be!

When the doctor released me, Dave took me back to the little prison apartment made to look like an office and apartment building. The only thing good about it was that not only were there always bowls of fresh nuts and fruits and vegetables around, but there was a little ice chest filled with milk and juices. There were even some crackers and cheese and a jar of peanut butter and one of jelly, and a loaf of bread. I ate continuously. Almost, the more I ate the more I wanted, which was strange since when I came in food really wasn't that important to me.

The first day Dave talked to me for hours, but I turned him off the way Sky had taught us to do. None of the words he said got past my eardrums. I guess in a way it was self-hypnosis because while I wasn't able to concentrate as completely on things of the Kingdom as I could during Purim meditation, I could still block out what Dave was saying while at the same time I was inwardly semi-reinforcing myself. We'd all been taught about deprogrammers, and been scared silly by some of the methods they might use.

On the second day Dave got a little more physical. He made me sit in a chair and look at him. He kept distracting me and breaking my astro connections by first screaming at me and then a few minutes later splashing drops of ice water in my face and things like that. I couldn't concentrate on Purim meditation. His Satan vileness, against my will, kept sinking into my mind. Dave kept repeating that Sky was the deceiver. I wouldn't believe it, but I couldn't shut it out.

On the third day I tried to wrap my head in my arms or put my hands over my ears so I wouldn't have to listen to Dave's blasphemy. I tried to control my mind with Purim meditation, astro connection, even transcendental meditation, which Sky said was the primer of the arts, but I couldn't! I couldn't control Dave's voice and his thoughts. They plummeted at me like rocks, some of them bruising me, hurting me. And he didn't care!

I wouldn't hurt him like he was hurting me, and then I remembered, I would! Maybe a little later I'd have to! I tried to recall everything that Sky and Trust had told me. First Jesus had said life was filled with both goats and sheep and Jesus had divided us. We, as sheep, were allowed, without guilt or punishment, to take what we needed or wanted, or to use the goats in any way without guilt or punishment. They were only sacrificial things anyway. Dave, along with Mom and Frank and all the other goats were only allowed existence temporarily until the great sifting and burning when they would be given to Satan to do with as he pleased. Nothing I could do to them would be so bad as what Satan would do! Days and nights got mixed up, and I didn't know how long Dave had been hammering at me. Sometimes I wanted to kill him or myself because he made me have moments of doubt about Sky and his Kingdom.

Was it true that by working us all as slaves he had, in his few years as a cult leader, amassed millions of dollars, which he had deposited in Swiss banks? And that only two months before my leaving, he had leased a lavish apartment in one of the most exclusive buildings in a town four hours drive from the Kingdom, where he had ordered an open channel for pornographic films, and where he was visited by the youngest and kinkiest of whores? I wouldn't believe it even when Dave showed me Xeroxed statements of bank balances and business dealings and pictures of Sky walking into a fashionable building in the dudiest of clothes with a little sex kitten hanging on each arm. They had rigged those things. I had heard about low lifes like that. I wouldn't believe it. I wouldn't! I wouldn't! I wouldn't! But seeds of doubt had been planted. During the daytime I could retain my faith in Sky's Kingdom and our Jesus people. At night little black fears haunted me. But I couldn't give in! I had been dedicated and consecrated to Jesus. Jesus was not wrong! Never in this or any of the worlds to come could Dave convince me He was! But Sky . . . I wept. Oh please, Jesus, don't let any of the things this Son of Satan is saying be true.

For a few days my mind became so messed up I couldn't tell reality from unreality. Sometimes I thought I was still with Sky. Sometimes I thought I was with Jesus. Sometimes Dave seemed like Trust, and one time he even appeared to be Dawn who was dead. I had lost my mind. Maybe the whole experience had been the hallucinations of a disillusioned and neurotically weak mind. Then Dave would appear from nowhere, verbally hammering . . . hammering . . . hammering. I pleaded with him to leave me alone. I had to get some rest. I was exhausted, confused, frightened. Would my mind ever work again, or would I be a permanent resident at a funny farm, or one of those slobbering sad lumps one sees from time to time wandering blank-eyed, lonely, and untouchable around the streets? Every town and city had one or two. Oh, dear, dear Jesus, please don't let me be one of them, I pleaded.

One day after Dave had worn me down to admitting that I really didn't know anything for sure, I remembered Jesus and countered, "I know Jesus lives, you can kill me but you'll never get me to deny that." I began to scream, "How can you hate Jesus so?"

Dave's voice was barely audible as he curled up on the floor beside me and tenderly took my hand. "I love Jesus," he choked.

"You can't love him."

"I love him as much as you do."

"No, no, no."

"Yes, yes, yes."

"Then how can you say what you say?"

"One of the reasons is because I can't stand by and let people like Sky and all the other cult leaders throughout the country make a mockery of Him."

"That's a lie."

"No, it's not."

"Yes, it is! You're trying to crucify Jesus again, and kill me, or, worse than that, make me lose control of my mind."

"Sky has already done that."

"You're crazy. Sky taught me and protected me and . . ."

He shook me hard. "Sometime you've got to face the fact that Sky is the only thing that's blowing your mind."

"He helped me find myself and my eternal destiny."

"He used you."

"He helped me find love and peace for myself and all mankind."

"Love? What did he teach you about your parents? What did he say about the Ten Commandments? Especially the one that says 'Honor thy Father and thy Mother'?"

"Well. . . ."

"Well, what? Are you going to believe Sky or the Bible?"

"He could explain that."

Dave's voice became hard and cold, "Like he explained having you sleep like mice, and eat barely enough to exist, and work like you weren't even human while he spent Friday, Saturday, and Sunday of each week in his luxurious apartment being treated like an oriental potentate."

"That's not true. He loved us."

"The doorman has sworn that he has spent Friday, Saturday, and Sunday of each week at his apartment for the past two months."

I had to protect Sky. Still, he had left early Friday morning for the past two months and come home late Sunday night long after all of us were asleep. There had to be some explanation.

It's funny how I finally broke. I had been resisting Dave's efforts to deprogram me for . . . I'd lost track of time. Then one day as I sat flossing my teeth with Dave hovering over me hammering at me, out of the blue I said, "There was no excuse for Sky not to buy me dental floss, was there?"

Dave came over and hugged me.

"I've always liked shiny, clean teeth, they make me feel shiny and clean both outside and in. Sky said to be really Christlike we must give up all things of the world except the barest necessities. He never said I couldn't buy dental floss, but I'd have felt so guilty if I had spent money on something as frivolous as that, I'd have been sure I'd be forever a damned and lost soul—an unworthy follower."

Dave laughed, "If you asked Jesus for dental floss, do you think He'd give it to you?"

I began to laugh in the first time that I could remember.

"I know it."

"And your parents?"

"Oh, yes!"

"And me?"

I continued to gurgle inside with that nice warm feeling that laughter brings. "Of course you would. Even rotten, old, mean, cantankerous, always-hacking-away you would buy me dental floss."

The next day I found with the fresh fruit, an electric toothbrush with twelve shiny new inserts in every color, and twelve boxes of unwaxed floss. It was the start of my recovery, which took a long time, and has left many holes to be mended in my past and I'm sure in my future, but I'm working on it. I'm taking just this semester of high school and then I'll take the College Equivalency test so I won't have to make up the full year I lost while I was in the cult.

Oh, dear Jesus, I wish it were lost, that somehow, some way I could lose it, but it's like a nightmare that keeps popping up at inopportune moments. Like my sacred Third Kingdom name; I still haven't been able to reveal it to anyone. Dave said he understands, and he's the only one who knows how I feel about it, but I don't understand. I wish I did. Maybe someday I will. Anyway, Sky was right about one thing: "If one lives in the past, there's no way one can progress into their future."

MARK
the lure of suicide

As I think about the whole a-hole concept of life, I wonder if it's worth the struggle. Man, what a grind, what a hassle.

It never used to be this way. I remember when I was a little kid, life was so exciting I couldn't wait from one day to the next to see what was going to happen. Like the time we made our Christmas home movie . . . the dad-gummed donkey we borrowed from someone wouldn't go, and little May, with her front stuffed with rags so she'd look pregnant, had to get down off him and help Tim, as Joseph, pull the stubborn thing. And when Lee, as King Herod, called for the dancing girls, Todd and me, in just our tight pajama bottoms and our Mom's bracelets, went and got Tiffany and Julie Ann, who were bedangled with all the scarves in our whole combined community. Man, that was funny, them feeding nine-year-old

King Herod grapes and shaking their little "boo-
dies."

Now, every Christmas when we see the film,
we all crack up; but we're impressed, too, because
it was a special time, and Christmas still is. Well,
it usually is except that one Christmas when I was
about ten and Mom got sent to the psychiatric
ward of the State Medical School. Man, what a
bummer. I still sometimes have nightmares thinking about the blackness and loneliness of it. I
guess it was about in October that she started
becoming depressed, or at least so damned down-
depressed that she couldn't function. At first Dad
started yelling and nagging at her because she
slept most of the day instead of doing her
housework and fixing meals and stuff. Then he
even started punching her out occasionally. Oh,
he never broke any bones or blacked her eyes or
anything, but I still wanted to kill him. I'd come
home from school and try to do things myself so
he wouldn't be mad, but I always made things
worse, like putting red socks in with all the white
clothes. When Dad saw his pink boxers, he about
blew the roof off the house. Often, long after I
should have been asleep I could hear him tossing
Mom around in their room and telling her she
was a failure even in bed. Man, what a grosser.
I remember trying to figure out all the details
about that, but at that age, what the hell, I didn't

know what was really coming off.

But Dad is neat, too. He took me sailing and water skiing and tried to make me his buddy. I guess he needed a friend, but I didn't want to be his friend. I wanted to be his son. I wanted to be protected, and loved, and made secure—just as I knew Mom did. I guess I related more to her than to him . . . her needing someone to care, and nobody did, except me, and I didn't really count. Katie was too little to be more than confused and no help to anyone at all.

Mom, who had always been the neatest artist in the world, and I'm sure could have become famous if she hadn't decided to get married and have a family, started painting weird things, things so bad it made me sick to my stomach to look at them—portraits of herself looking like the very damned in the lowest pits of hell, her eyes so filled with sorrow and pain that even looking at the portraits made me go to my room and shut myself in my closet and cry. I'd cry until I felt like dry rocks were coming out of my eyes and my insides were like they'd been worked over by six mix masters filled with broken glass. But who the hell cared about me? They were too busy caring about themselves.

In November, Dad, who hadn't wanted any of the relatives to know about Mom, finally gave up and called Grandpa in Dallas and asked if we could come and stay with them for a few weeks. Of course they said yes and came right in to get us. It was kind of neat. Grandpa took me to the Father-and-Son's Scouting party, and it was really fun.

But I missed Dad. I needed him. Lee and Doug had their Dad, and Tim and Todd did too. I wanted mine. Oh, I loved Grandpa, and he teased me and loved me and everything, but I guess every guy needs a Dad.

At home Dad took me to do the things he wanted me to do but not the things I wanted to do, like he was gung-ho about sailing and basketball and took me to the "Y" and had me join a team and stuff. But I'm not really all that coordinated and I always felt the team would have been better off without me. And with water skiing and stuff, he thought it was weird that I really would have been happier at home reading or watching TV shows or playing with my games or writing.

I was in the middle of writing the script for our next home movie. It was going to be an outer space thing with Lee, and Tim, and Todd and me eating or kidnapping all the girls. Lee and me were both writing it, and it was going to be a smash—bigger even than "The Horse Thieves" or "The Lost Colt" or "The Christmas Movie,"— the three other movies we had all put together.

Dad didn't understand that. He thought I was a sissy because I didn't like his things, but at least I tried to do them and make him happy. Man, how I tried! I suffered over trying to score baskets and make him proud of me on water skis like I've never suffered over anything before or since. I concentrated and commanded my muscles and relaxed and everything the coach told me to do. I tried so hard and so seriously it was hardly ever any real fun except, I guess, sometimes. Actually, when I was waterskiing behind the boat with spray swishing out like wings I really felt like I was gonna soar right off the earth and up into some wonderful secret place beyond. That was fantastic! and actually was really the feeling I was always looking for when I started doping, but I didn't find it.

For a few months one summer Dad and Uncle Greer got to be good friends, and all of us guys would go fishing some Saturdays. It was neat, my friends and me in the reeds making traps when we got tired of fishing. We never did catch anything, but we sure made some fine and complicated contraptions. Then someone stole Dad's fishing equipment and we never did go back. Grandpa offered to lend us his, but Dad never could go any way but the best, so we didn't go. I tried to pretend it didn't make me no never mind, but it did! When Mom was sick, it was kind of like we were living in two worlds. At Grandpa's and Grandma's they couldn't do enough for us, and they were always trying to think of things we'd like to do and what we'd like to eat.

The only time Grandpa ever quarreled with Dad was when Dad insisted on taking us to the hospital to see Mom. Dad could take her out every day; Grandpa wanted us to meet at home. But Mom and Dad, who had always felt if they had any fights or anything they should be in front of us, said it wouldn't hurt us to see Mom in the "crazy house." That isn't exactly what Dad said, but it's what me and Katie both thought. We only knew about people being locked up for being crazy from TV shows and that was pretty gruesome. I didn't want to go myself and I sure as hell didn't want my poor little hurty sister to go. Maybe some crazy inmate would try to grab her, or lock her in his cage with him or something, or maybe they'd do it to me.

Grandma heard me crying in my sleep one night and tried to explain to me how it really was when someone was locked up in a mental hospital because they're depressed, and I felt some better because I knew she didn't lie. It was just to protect Mom so that she wouldn't commit suicide, and the doctor had started giving her something so she'd get out of her depressed mood. Grandma and Grandpa both went often to see her and they kept telling me it wasn't all that bad there, but they still didn't want us to go. So it must have been kind of bad. Mom was there for a month and each Saturday Dad took her out to dinner with us, but she was always anxious to go back. It was like she felt safer there than with us.

One day Dad got mad at Grandpa again and took us home. It was lonely, and I started thinking maybe Mom was right, maybe life wasn't worth living. The more I thought about it, the more convinced I became that life was just one big pile of shit. When Grandma called I told her how I felt, and the next thing I knew she was in Fort Worth packing our duds.

I expected Dad to blow all the batteries from kingdom come, but he didn't. He even seemed relieved when he talked to us on the phone.

As I think back I really appreciate all the concentrated effort Grandma put forth to change my attitude. She made a little face to hang on the fireplace. On one side it was smiling, and on the other side frowning, and without constantly reminding me, she turned it from one side to the other as my moods changed. It really helped a lot and reminded me to be happy and look for the good things like she said.

One night Grandpa brought out a bunch of Bibles and we all took turns reading any part we liked to each other. It was fun for Katie and me to find a part we could understand, and one she could read. Sometimes, even when I didn't get the meaning, just doing it made me feel good inside.

One Sunday we went to Sunday School and I remember that me, and L.J., and Tommy Joe sat on the back row of the class and punched each other and giggled, and got scolded by the teacher and even made to sit with the girls. It still was a good inside feeling. I wished Mom and Dad would take us every Sunday like my friends' parents. But Mom and Dad didn't believe in God. They'd lived in New York for years, and Dad had been kind of a wheel in advertising, and I guess they just thought . . . I don't know what they thought. . . . But I remember they used to say that they believed what they wanted to believe and we could, too.

Well, I guess Mom wasn't sick for all that long. A month doesn't seem like that much time now, but then it seemed forever and ever—wondering, hoping, being glad Grandma and Grandpa had sent me to church and taught me enough so I knew how to pray.

I still get mad at my parents when I think of them making me feel guilty because I wanted to pray, but I'm sure in their own way they were, and still are, doing what they think is best for us.

It's too bad that no one explained to us when

Mom was sick that thousands, probably hundreds of thousands of people, go through the same thing she went through. That sometimes it's a chemical condition in the body and other times it's just brought on by stress and pressures. I've tried to analyze Mom's case as I've gotten older and I think hers was mostly stress. Dad always made her, like everyone else, feel unimportant.

Anyway, Mom left Dad shortly after she was released from the hospital; maybe her psychiatrist recommended it, I don't know. Parents never tell kids anything. We're the last to know, if we ever find out at all.

It hurt me a lot that Mom left us. I guess I really wanted Dad to leave and her to come home and take care of the house and us and stuff, but like she said one time, there was no way she could possibly have done that. It was all she could do to handle a small apartment and take care of herself on the grubby little salary she made as a window decorator and display artist in a department store. It was a weird arrangement after the separation, her coming over to sit with us while Dad went out on dates and them trying like hell to be friends and all that shit.

Then Dad ran across bad times in business, and we kids came home and took care of ourselves till he returned home at night. Sometimes he'd call me and Katie and tell us what to put on for dinner.

It was the shits. And besides that, he was always talking about moving back to New York where he could be a big shot again. That always spooked me because I never have made friends easy. It's hard to make good friends, especially dependable, forever-type friends like I had in Dallas and Fort Worth.

Well, somehow the next four years slid by. I'd feel upped when I went to my grandparents, protected and secure, but kind of floating on an unknown stream of life when I was home, never knowing at which minute we'd run into white water, or be tossed against the rocks, or thrown over waterfalls or whatever. Sometimes I'd have bad dreams about it and I wished I had someone to talk to, but I didn't. Life wasn't worth diddly.

When I was in my second year of junior high, I started getting into dope pretty good. At first it sounded like the perfect way to escape, but uppers weren't for me. I got so nervous and paranoid I couldn't concentrate on anything and I started taking out all my hostilities on Katie and threatening that if she told Mom or Dad I'd punch her out so good she'd never tell anybody anything else.

Poor little kid. One day when I was unstoned I saw what I was really doing to her. She was so scared of me she pulled away and blinked every time I even came close. Ashamed of myself, I broke down and the two of us clung together like Hansel and Gretel, or whoever it was in the fairy story that got lost in the woods and were afraid the witch was going to eat them. What a butt I'd been, even more selfish and thinking only of myself than Mom and Dad. Poor, poor little eleven-year-old Katie. Whatever in hell did life have in store for her. I vowed I'd never use uppers again; they made me too mean and easily upset.

The next few months passed with just more of the same, except that I found religion. That sounds like a weird thing to say for a fifteen-year-old kid, but I really did. I was sitting in church one night with Grandpa and this real good, kind feeling came over me that I wanted to keep with me forever. It was like peace and love and security, and all the brilliantly light things I'd ever needed and wanted. I didn't want the meeting to ever end, didn't want to leave that nice safe comfortable feeling. But it did end and Katie and me went back home to more days and nights and weeks of the garbage leftovers of both Mom and Dad's lives. In a way, instead of helping me "having gotten religion" made it harder. I began to resent my parents' always having taken us to PG movies and anything else they wanted to see, leaving sex books and stuff around for us if we wanted to look at them, having booze and cigarettes always available when we wanted to use them—not that we did to their faces, but I'm sure they both knew we did behind their backs. And crude language! If they or their friends hadn't said it, it wasn't being used. Not that my friends, by then, were any little Holy Rollies, but you expect kids to be . . . I dunno.

Katie and I were still doing well in school. We'd both always been good students, and I was proud of her. She'd always been really aggressive. Every time something happened, she'd stand up to it and fight, a real little hellcat. But me, well I guess I'm just more of a quitter. I used to think I was a diplomat, trying to please Mom, and then Dad, and my teachers, and everybody else in the world until I found it just made every day of the week "walk on me" day, so I just started to retreat. Shit, I couldn't please or make any of them happy anyway. Thank God for books and TV. What did the aborigines ever do without them? Man, I'm as hooked on game shows and the soaps as I could ever be on dope. They're my life. Sometimes I think Doctor Hardy and Peter and his wife and kids are almost more my family than my own. When Steve found out it was his kid that had shot himself through the head, it was just like it had happened to me and I began fantasizing about what would have happened if it really had been me. Not so many people would have cared, or cared so deeply, but it sure was neat and I sure could relate. I don't know what I'll ever do if they put me on the late lunchtime so I'd miss it. Guess I'd just have to cut that class.

We spent the last weekend at Grandma's before we moved back to New York. I was so filled with hate and anger and anguish I felt like a stick of dynamite about to go off. Katie and me begged Dad not to go. We didn't want to leave our friends and our school and everything . . . even Mom. She said maybe she'd move back there later, but shit, we needed her now. Katie especially needed her now, and I needed her. What a sucking baby I was; I wanted my Mama. I wanted her home to make cookies and read stories and clean and nag at me and . . . oh crap, if she only knew the pain. Did she feel it, too? Did anyone except me, and maybe Katie? I needed someone home when I came in from school. The house was so quiet and cold and sterile and lonely. Sometimes when Katie stayed at a friend's, or at school for something, I would wander through the rooms just calling quietly, "Mom . . . Mom . . ." like I used to when I was a little kid, half expecting her to come out from somewhere and grab me in her arms and snuggle me down tight and securely so nothing bad could ever happen to me again in my whole lifetime. That just showed what a big baby butt I was! Maybe I'd just cut out and stay

here or become a street kid. I wondered how that
would be? Then I could stay home and watch TV
all day and read, and smoke pot when I didn't
want to do that.

But I wouldn't have a TV and where would I
get bread for . . . oh, crap, I was so unrealistic.

I asked Dad if we couldn't just live with our
grandparents for awhile, but he said he needed us.
Nothing about our needs, what we cared about,
what we wanted! Gramps took me on a scouting
trip once, and we really had a good time, but Jay
Walker and me were the only ones without Dads.
Jay went with Brother Ohran, the scoutmaster,
and of course I was with Gramps, but even that's
not really the same. Man, I really felt like a little
sissy crybaby when I lay down in my sleeping bag
and sobbed while the other kids and their Dads
whispered, but somehow I knew Grandpa understood and that made it some better.

I couldn't expect Dad to give up his whole life
for us, and I knew the opening in New York
would be a big step up for him again, and we'd
have a maid and a nice apartment on 63rd and all
that. But . . . well, I'd miss living on the outskirts
in a semirural area and I'd miss . . . but I wouldn't
if Dad would get into the scouting program.
Maybe even that was different there; maybe the
kids and Dads wouldn't . . . I guessed they
wouldn't because Lee and Tim's troup was

through their church, and everything there was strictly family oriented. I didn't know how my Mom could have given up all that beauty and truth and togetherness. She didn't believe any of it any more, even about Jesus and God, and that hurt me. It was like saying the sun doesn't come up and shine when I could see it with my very own eyes, and feel its warmth and power on my skin, and see how it made things grow and blossom and . . . oh shit, I'm sounding like a sucking baby again.

Sitting around a campfire with your Dad is what it's all about. Fishing and working and playing. Loving your neighbor, loving your family, trying to make the world a better place. Not just money or prestige . . . not that they're not important . . . but I don't know, it just seems my parents had got their priorities all screwed up.

New York City was the pits. Everyone had their mouths full of shit and their language was so foul I couldn't even believe it. Things me and my friends used to talk about in the bushes you heard about all over. The first day I was in the hall and heard a girl say to some guy, "Hey, Gary, you wanna come over tonight and ball?" I almost lost my sox. She said it just like you'd say, "Wanna come over and watch TV?" And she wasn't just some nothing ugly chick that looked like she'd run into a parked car. She was a fancy fox that dressed in leather pants and stuff and was in my starred English class. She was one of the brains. I'd had the hots for her myself until that incident; then she kind of turned my stomach.

The second day at school the kid in the next gym locker offered me some Reds and I took them happily, anything to get a friend. During lunch we sat on the steps and grooved. I'd never used downers before and man, they were for me —no jumping-out-of-my-skin feelings, just slowed down, restful, semifloating. I could cope in my classes and still not be bugged by anything or anyone in the whole world. I hadn't wanted Ted to think I was a greenie; so I'd pretended to take two and had only taken one, but man, that's all the nice I needed. I remember the thought kept floating over and over again in my head like a sweet stuck record, "I wanna stay on . . . on . . . on . . . on . . . on . . . on . . . on all the rest of my life."

And it wasn't all that hard. Reds cost about seventy-five cents apiece, and it only took five a day to keep me in that restful atmosphere, where nothing or nobody on earth could hurt or harm or upset me. But even five began to be a hassle: $3.75 a day, $26.25 a week, $105.00 a month, before I bought hamburgers or candy bar number one. That might present a problem.

I asked Teddy about getting a job as a box boy or a paper boy or something. He just laughed. "Kids in cities can't work," he told me, "it's against the law—child labor and all that garbage. They gotta work for the 'Midnight Auto Supply,' or the corner 'Ripoff Station.' "

Well, at first I dragged my feet. I didn't feel good about stealing. I'd squeeze the old man as long as possible and maybe something else would come up. It did. Saturday, when I was down in the basement of our apartment building washing my tennies and dirty gym clothes, one of the ladies in the building came down to do her laundry, too. At first she just smiled and looked me over. I thought maybe she had a kid my age or something. "I love the smell of your gym clothes," she said, friendly as if she'd known me forever.

"My Mother never did," I smiled back, thinking maybe I'd found a nice Mother-image friend who I could talk to about all the things that were bugging the shit out of me when I wasn't stoned, which wasn't often.

She came over and picked up my sweat shirt and buried her face in it, "Oh, macho, macho," she whispered. "Kids are so much more macho than men."

I was embarrassed and tried to take it away from her, vowing I was going to buy some deodorant the first thing. This lady was putting me on like my Mother used to sometimes. Mom would come in when my room looked like a bomb had just gone off and she'd tell me how proud she was that I was so neat and organized and stuff; then we'd sit in the hall and roll with laughter.

Man, what a neat, neat feeling—until the lady picked up my boxers and my jockstrap. She looked me straight in the eye, "Wanna screw?" she asked.

I almost choked. Blood gushed up to my head till I was waiting for the thunder of it to erupt through my ears, my eyeballs, and even the top of the soft spot in my head, like a volcano.

"Baby, wanna screw Mama?" she asked again softly, like maybe I wanted to borrow some soap or something.

I wanted to run and hide, kill myself, anything . . . but then I thought . . . Oh, what the hell, I was a big boy and I had to learn some time. But she was like my Mother. When I looked close I could see that she was older than my Mother . . . little lines dug deep into her skin around her eyes almost like my Grandmother's. Wouldn't that be embarrassing seeing her naked?

The blood started flowing back down to the parts she was interested in, and nothing else mattered any more.

She told me which apartment she was in and asked me to come up a couple of minutes after she left.

I wanted to cut out forever. But where the hell would I go? What the hell would I do? I wished I had a church or a minister or . . . anybody. Something in the back of my head kept hammering about adultery was breaking one of the Ten Commandments, but you had to be married to commit adultery, didn't you? It was like being stoned, my mind tripping all over itself . . . I wanted to but I didn't want to . . . Was it because it was the first time? I wasn't married so I couldn't commit adultery.

Oh shit, how I wished I had a handful of Reds, but I had run out. Maybe my parents were right. Maybe church just did confuse people, make them feel guilty about the things that were normal. I was drawn up to Elisha's apartment like a pin is drawn to a magnet, or a moth is drawn to a light. I didn't want to go, I really didn't . . . but I did.

After it was over, I felt filthy and degraded. I'd been like a dumb animal in heat once I'd gotten involved. I didn't care about her or the Ten Commandments or anything. I just cared about me. Maybe that was what sex was all about, just self-gratification. She hadn't been a person or anything special at all, just a thing that gave me a temporary feeling that was, well, . . . disgusting.

When it was over, I was so exhausted I stumbled back to our apartment and puked; then I drank a whole water glass full of Dad's bourbon. I hated myself. I hated life. But I hated Elisha the most. If that was love . . . but I didn't want to remember; I wanted to forget, escape, forever, forever, forever! I started into the bathroom to get Dad's bottle of sleeping pills, but passed out in the hall before I got there.

A few days later I saw Elisha in the elevator as I was going down to school. I backed off and took the next one. She was waiting in the lobby for me and while she didn't speak, as she walked by she slipped something into my jacket pocket. I hoped it would be a note saying she felt as bad as I did, but it wasn't. It was a fifty dollar bill. I wanted to tear it up in little pieces and mix it with spit and throw it in her face, but she was gone. So I went out and bought myself a supply of Reds. Life was pretty unbearable without them. Booze was better than nothing, but it never would be my thing.

I met a girl at school I liked, Sandy. She lived over by Bloomy's. We took the bus to and from school every day and ate lunch together and even met between classes. It was wonderful. Having someone, belonging. We talked about anything and everything for hours, everything except Elisha.

She kept asking me what I was holding back, but I couldn't tell her. I didn't want her to think I was an animal. I wanted to protect her and care for her tenderly, to feel myself a man, concerned about others and their feelings, their desires, their needs. Sometimes I'd kiss her and we'd make out a little, but that was it.

When I began to feel that Sandy was getting suspicious about my manhood, I told her I had vowed as part of my religion that I would be a virgin when I got married. She liked that and our relationship became even stronger. We made long-range programs, goals for our high school years, our college years, when we would be married, what kind of parents we would be, about values and priorities. It was fulfilling and comforting, much better than sex. And we were going to be such fantastically loving and caring parents. Her parents were divorced, too. In fact her Dad had been married twice, her Mom three times and now was living with the vice-president of the company she worked for. Everybody thought it was a real neat arrangement, everybody but Sandy; she was embarrassed that her Mother wasn't married. She said it made her feel illegitimate, which didn't make any sense at all, but I understood. It was kind of like adults live on the surface, with no roots, or anything important or stable. Sometimes I wondered if I was crazy because I needed those

things so much and longed for them so desperately, but I figured I wasn't, because Sandy felt the
same way. We were so good for each other. I
could see why young kids get into physical relationships; they need someone to help them and
stand by them so desperately and parents didn't
anymore. Sandy and I both wished we had lived
during times when families were real things.

Sandy went through her rough years when she
was eleven and twelve. One of her Mother's boyfriends raped her regularly for about a month and
threatened her if she told—so she went through
the hogwash, too. She told me about the other
guys she'd known and we were really trying hard
to equate sex with love. We decided that until we
did, it just was not for us. Sometimes we got kind
of close, but I guess we were both too uptight. I
guess really we were afraid, afraid we'd lose that
wonderful—whatever—we had if we let sex into
our relationship, which is kind of sick thinking in
itself because sex and love are what it's supposed
to be all about. "Multiply and replenish the
earth" was the first commandment in the Garden
of Eden. Maybe that was the secret. Maybe we
could find all the answers in church. Oh, what a
wonderful, wonderful feeling, the church, and
Sandy, and love and me all as one. I couldn't wait
for the two of us to go together and talk to a priest
or father or minister or somebody. And this was

the time to. We were both straight, working hard in school, trying to do all the things our parents didn't give a shit if we did or not. We'd got our heads together and we were really ready for the next step up.

I wondered if I'd ever be able to look Sandy in the face again. She and her Mother and stud went away for the holiday. For the first two days I worried myself sick about her, then I accidentally got in the elevator with Elisha, rather I was in the elevator when she got in. I wanted to escape through the loudspeaker or the heat vent or something . . . anything, but I couldn't. Her perfume was overpowering, and when she reached over and put her hands on my . . . my . . . well, it was like I was stoned completely out of my tree.

I can't believe the movies she showed, or the junk we took, or the things we did, and the way we talked.

All the hostility I had ever had, or ever would have, poured out of me, and Elisha said she "loved" it. I remember screaming when I thought about that word "love." It was all so bizarre that I lost my mind and went into the most violent, sickening bummer trip any mortal could ever have. I don't know how I reached my own apartment, I only know that the next four days I spent in bed, shivering and whimpering. Dad poked his head in a couple of times and told me not to worry, "The flu is like that." Then he went about his own business.

I'm sure little Katie knew more than she let on. But what could she do? She was even more trapped and helpless than I was.

Lorna Jo, the maid who came in on Tuesday and Friday, had to come on Thursday. Dad had insisted that she change so she could be there while I was sick. She let me know nonverbally what a pain in the butt I was to her, how much I'd inconvenienced her while she was trying to clean, and how rough it was to fix me a bowl of soup. It sure the hell didn't make me no never mind. I wanted to kill them both and myself before the day was over. I wondered how the apartment would burn, if I could electrocute myself in the microwave oven. Booze and pills hadn't worked. How about a razor?

On Friday I was feeling shaky but sane. I knew I had to talk to someone about Elisha. She had made me lose all respect for myself and for everything else—simply everything in the whole world. Every time I passed a drugstore window and saw the cosmetic products her company manufactured, I wanted to barf.

On Sunday I screwed up the courage to ask Dad to talk to me. Helplessly bubbling over with terror and tears, I tried to explain how I had gotten involved with Elisha. But before I could get past what had happened in the laundry room, he started laughing and fluffing me off, telling me older women were the best teachers, that I'd sure picked a foxy older chick for myself, and that he wondered what she'd seen in a punk like me when she could have had a real stallion like him.

The dam collapsed inside me and I knew there was no way he would understand. I lay awake for nights afterwards wondering if his relationships were with women like Elisha. What was normal? What was acceptable? I knew beating and brutalness weren't, but what about the other stuff? Where did right and acceptable begin and end?

I wished I were a eunuch. If I hadn't been such a sissy, I would have made myself one.

On Thursday I found two crisp one-hundred dollar bills in my English book. I went straight to one of the school dealers. Reds seemed to be the only way to make life bearable.

Sandy hung on me and begged me to talk to her, but what could I say? I started using two Reds instead of one. My only worry was how I would replenish my supply once they were gone.

Saturday I was stretched out on my bed enjoying the dots on the ceiling, when Katie tiptoed into my room. Her tears wet my face as she talked about how things had always been with us, how much we'd loved each other even when we'd fought. And she brought up things I couldn't even remember—about how I'd protected her when some kids were chasing her home from school once, and stuff. I wished I wasn't so spaced out so I could relate better with her, but I couldn't. She droned on and on about how close we'd been, and I wanted so much to show my appreciation to her that I pulled out the drawer of my chest and offered her a Red. At first her eyes opened wide; then I told her how neat it would make her feel and she sat down in the chair beside me and "took off." I remember thinking we were one again like we had been when we were little kids sharing the sandbox. "What a neat little sister. What a neat little sister," I kept saying over and over again. After a while she joined me in a slowed-down voice, "What a neat, always-for-eternity type brother. What a neat . . . always . . . for . . . e . . . ter . . . nity . . ."

Hours later I woke up. Katie was curled up in the chair with her feet on the bed under my head. She looked exactly like she had when she was about seven, tiny and fragile, vulnerable and helplessly kittenlike. What had I done? Eleven years old and I, her own brother who should be protecting her, introducing her to dope. What a butt I was! What a contemptible no-good butt!

I sat down and wrote a short note:

Dear little sister:

Please do not get involved in drugs and sex. They can only bring you unhappiness and pain. Stay good and be happy. I will write you when I get my head together.

I couldn't write "love," it was such a misused word; so I finished, "You always have been and always will be the sunshine of my life." Then I signed it by our private pet name, "Markoronovitchiski." Oh, how I lo . . . cherished that precious little kid! How I wanted only the good in life for her!

After I'd packed my duffle bag, I bent and kissed her gently on the cheek. Precious, innocent little baby! Wouldn't anyone take care of her and protect her and lo . . . God—like kind of love her.

The streets were still and eerie as I started down Lexington. At five-thirty in the morning in New York City even the muggers had gone in for the night. I didn't know where I was going only that I wanted to go south. I needed some sunshine and warmth in my soul, as well as on my physical body.

I had cleaned out Dad's wallet. Would $197 get me to California or Arizona or Nevada? How long would it take before the blood got thawed out in my veins?

How would Dad and Katie take it when they found I had cut out? I knew she'd cry and feel bad. Probably he'd just tell her how he'd run away, too, when he was my age. But he'd just run away to a relative's ranch to work for the summer. I had no place to go. None of my relatives had ranches and the ones I'd like to go to had big enough families, so they didn't need one more mouth to feed. Especially they didn't need someone who'd be such a bad example as I'd be to their own kids.

Mom had married some dude who was an artist, and they were going around selling their paintings in shopping malls and stuff. They didn't need me hanging around getting in their way. Clodhopper, clumsy, uncoordinated me, I'd probably have them at each other's throats as soon as I got there.

Crap, it was time I saw what the world was like for myself anyway. And it didn't make any difference if I never did go back to junior high or high school. I could practically pass the College Equivalency test without even trying now; one of my counselors had told me so. Maybe I could just happen by schools in different cities each year and rip off the books they studied from and I'd be more educated than most kids even without school.

Shit, I didn't know how cozy and protected I had
had it at home. The first trucker I rode with took
me to Pittsburgh and all the way talked about
gross things so sickening I'd have jumped out at
the first stop, except it was so damned cold outside
I'd probably have frozen to death before anyone
else would have picked me up. So I just "ya'd"
him and "sure . . . sure'd" him till he came to a
truck stop to fill up. By then he was calling me
"little buddie," and on his CB unit was telling
some guy I guess he knew how he had a new
"little buddie" and what "fun we was going to
have." But I kept saying to myself, "no way man."
I was gonna ditch as soon as I could find some
protection from the damned storm.

I stayed in the restaurant until he pulled out.
Then I started sizing guys up, listening to what
they talked about; I wasn't gonna get caught with
another degenerate turkey.

One guy in the restaurant was talking about
how anxious he was to get home to his wife and
kids, and about his littlest one, who'd just had a
pretty serious operation of some kind, which was
why he was driving an extra shift or something.
He sounded like almost human, so I hit him up for
a ride to Kansas, which was where he was going.
He told me his company didn't allow them to pick
up riders, but . . . pretending to tell me "no," he
motioned me to the other side of the truck and

told me to slip in when no one was looking, including him.

That really kind of scared me because I had visions of him knocking me off out on some deserted stretch of road and then mutilating my body and tossing it out in clumps. Who'd ever know? What hurt even more was, how many people would care? Oh, Sandy would, and Katie would, and Mom and Dad would, too, and Grandma and Grandpa. Man, lots of people cared about me. I was just chicken shit and liver not to care about myself.

On the road me and Mike talked about that, how I didn't have any confidence and how important that was. He was one neat dude, telling me how his kids would never have a whole bunch of money and like that, but they sure had a lot of love. He told me how he met his wife in high school and how they'd been married fifteen years and he loved her more now than he did when they first met. It was really nice, barreling down the highway in a nice, cozy, warm truck cab, munching on candy bars, and fritos, and apples and junk he'd brought along, and talking about how life ought to be and how with him it really was. He said young people just fall in "like," and they don't really know what "love" is till they've weathered a few storms together and become one in a family through their combined sorrows, and frustrations and joys and accomplishments. It was almost like a sermon—actually better.

I was sorry I had told him I was going to Arizona to stay with my Mom because my Dad had lost his job. I would have liked visiting with him and his family and he'd even asked me too, but I couldn't back down because I knew his kids wouldn't lie. What would they have to lie about to someone as caring and understanding as he was?

He said their first kid had been born with a double cleft lip and a cleft palate, but that he was all right now after about six major operations and that he could do anything as good or better than anybody else in the whole world. Man, that made me feel great being with a Dad who just plain had that much confidence in his kid.

My Dad was always chopping me because I wasn't an ace in sports and other things he liked. I tried to pretend what it would be like to have a Father like Mike, but guessed I wouldn't like that either. I was positive that a truck driver couldn't make nearly as much money as an advertising executive, but crap, it sure would be nice to have a "building-up" kind of family.

I was sorry when we got to Kansas City, but Mike fixed me up to ride with an independent trucker friend of his who was going to Albuquerque, and I relaxed. Mike wouldn't have anyone he'd call a friend who was a real squid. Carl said he would be happy to have me with him because his relief trucker hadn't shown up. But I wasn't much help, and I just slept most of the way.

I couldn't believe it when we got to New Mexico. It was like going from winter to summer in three days. I just walked over to the nearest park and stretched out in the sun. Man, that was neat. It just fried right through me, kind of cooking all the impurities away. I felt like a new person, a new and clean and good person all ready to start over. But doing what? Where? How? I went to the YMCA and paid for two nights telling them my aunt was going to meet me, but I'd made a mistake and come in early, and I'd just have to wait because I didn't know how to get in touch with her since she'd just moved there. Man, I wasn't doing very well in other departments, but I sure was becoming a good liar.

Across the street from the "Y" was a funny little church, and I spent many hours in there meditating, trying to figure myself and other things out.

I half convinced myself that at least part of what I'd thought had happened at Elisha's had just been a bad trip. I'd always been the biggest of sissy chicken shits. I couldn't possibly have done some of the things I'd thought I'd done, even stoned on cannonballs or anything else.

I liked gentle things and gentle people. I'd never even had a fight with another guy, other than a couple of pushes and a few dirty words. Even the dirty words I'd hated, still hated; "shit" was about the only word you could even call gross that I ever used. My language was a lot cleaner than most adults I knew.

Not that I was trying to make myself out a Percy Pure or anything, but that just simply wasn't *me* on that Elisha trip. I wondered if the thoughts of it would ever go away, would ever dim. They were almost as vivid now as they'd been at the very first and I couldn't stand that. Every time the thoughts began to seep back into my mind I tried my very hardest to push them out, but it was almost like a flashback . . . maybe it was! Maybe she'd given me something that permanently damaged my mind. O God, not that, not my beautiful, wonderful mind, the thing I valued most highly in my life. I might not be much in sports and mechanics and stuff, but my mind . . . oh, God . . . please . . . please . . . not my mind.

I'd started reading when I was just barely five and by the time I was in third grade I could read almost anything in the library, and Katie was almost as good. That was the one area in my life in which I had any confidence. Oh, dear God, I couldn't have blown that.

My second day in town I met a couple of Hare

Krishna guys. They looked weird, but when I started talking to them they really seemed to know where it was at. Both of them had been like me, looking for something to believe in, to be dedicated too, something that would be a building and a "forever" experience. One kid's Father had been an alcoholic bum, never even able to keep food on the table. His Mom was a poor, not too smart, waddler addicted to the TV set. He was the youngest in the family and all the other kids had turned out to be bums, too, learning to steal food when they were young and anything else they wanted as they grew older. As I look back now, I think of how strange the two guys looked as they paraded down the streets with their shaven heads and orange robes over their regular street shoes and socks. They were selling junk and their robes ruffled out behind them like sprouting wings as they walked. We'd made fun of them in New York, but I didn't want to make fun of them in Albuquerque. They looked too calm and together, like I wanted to be.

The two took me to the raunchy little place where they lived and fed me, not fancy but filling stuff, and a couple of the other guys told me how rough it had been for them on the outs and how peaceful and fulfilled it was for them on the ins.

Ti's parents were wealthy and successful. His Father was a congressman, but nobody had any roots, they were all floaters, everybody trying to do and say what everybody else wanted them to do and say. He never knew who he really was because he'd been forced to live like a chameleon, always changing colors and personalities according to who was around. His sister, just older than him and in her second year of college, had driven off a bridge and killed herself. The papers said it was an accident and everybody believed that, or tried to, except Ti, who knew she'd gotten to the place where she just couldn't hack any more hypocrisy. She'd told him so and also that she was working on a plan to end it all that would be in true family tradition—a liar and hypocrite to the last curtain.

He said he hadn't cried for her at the funeral; instead he'd cried for all the phony wheels in attendance who could live with themselves in their dishonorable, manipulating, plastic vacuums. The day after the funeral he'd split to find something else.

Like me, he'd been scared and lonely and seeking till he'd found Hare Krishna. His voice broke and tears streamed down his face.

"This is right," he assured me, "I belong. People love me. I'm on an eternal quest to help—not harm, build—not tear down, love—not hate . . ." "Hare Krishna," they kept saying and I felt a comforting kind of protective love that I had only felt before in my life with my relatives and my very closest Texas friends.

I remembered Lee and me sleeping out on the lawn when we were little, talking all night about where we wanted to go and what we wanted to be when we grew up. How neat it was going to be when we were sixteen and could drive cars and stuff. That made my heart ache because I was almost there. Almost sixteen and old enough to drive a car, but where would I get one? I'd never have one if I stayed with the Hare Krishnas. They wanted only spiritual things, and I wasn't quite ready for that. I needed physical things, too. A car, a girl . . . a real young, sweet, nice girl like Sandy . . . maybe even a more protected girl . . . a virgin . . . and Lee and me double-dating. Yes, Lee and me and our dates going to drive-in movies or just cruising the streets, stopping at the A&W for hamburgers and stuff. The longing was a hurting thing, and I knew I had to go on.

I really missed the Hare Krishnas as I stood out on the lonely road waiting for some turkey to pick me up. And usually they were just that. The nice guys or families were too afraid that I might mug them and steal their cars like they had read about and seen on TV, and they were right. Most of the people I'd met on the road were bums just looking for something for nothing, or thinking the world owed them golden castles and silk sheets.

But maybe that wasn't fair because I'd only met a few of them. Maybe lots were like me . . . running to someplace . . . or from someplace . . . and not really knowing the difference.

Some long-haired young sicko in a van, who really thought he was hot snot, gave me a ride right out into the middle of the desert by Durango and pushed me out when I didn't want to slip in the back with him for "fun and games."

When I was half out of the car, he sicked his big old mongrel half-police, half-Doberman dog on me, and I thought for sure I was going to get torn to shreds, but sicko called him off just in time and tossing out the butt of his roach, peeled off down the lonely highway giving me the finger as he drove.

I crumpled up on the graveled shoulder and cried. Fifteen . . . almost sixteen . . . and sopping the front of my jacket and pants and the roadbed with tears, and shaking with sobs like I had convulsions. Life was really an a-hole place. People had to join weird close-your-eyes-and-don't-look-at reality orange-robed, head-shaven cults to save their sanity and their lives. But if everybody did that, who'd build the buildings, the bridges and cars, and supply the markets, and repair the telephones and TV's, and make clothes, and keep things progressing? Or was it progress? Maybe our civilizations throughout the world were just getting more and more like Sodom and Gomorrah in the Bible and like the ancient Greek and Roman cultures, so wicked and polluted that the only thing for God to do was to wipe them off the face of the earth, or let them degenerate into dusty ruins and start over again. I'd buy that! If a great atomic blast wiped out all the cultures of the world, and we had to start over again like the pioneers, we'd probably all be better off. Who needed TV's and books and . . . ? I did! I needed them! But pioneers had books. Everybody brought across the plains the things they personally cherished. I'd bring books, a whole wagonload full of them. And I'd meet a nice young girl, and we'd live like the family in *Little House on the Prairie* with only physical problems. Those we could handle.

The sun started burning hotter and hotter on my shoulders, but it felt good. If I died, it would at least be in sweet meditation. I wondered how long one could go on the desert without water. A day? Three days? The more I thought about it the thirstier I became. It was funny, but I wasn't sad. I was almost looking forward to dying. Who'd miss me? Would they even know who I was? I didn't think I had any identification. Would I just be one more John Doe in the morgue with a tag on my big toe like on TV? Anyway, I was glad I was going to die in the desert instead of in cold

New York or New Jersey. It was awful being cold
. . . but then it was miserable being too hot, too.

I got up and started walking in the direction the
van had gone. After a while the shiny brightness
started hurting my eyes and I began squinting.
When I squinted, I could see anything I wanted
to see stretching out in front of me: A&W root
beer stands, nice cozy little white cottages with
white picket fences and red roses and green yards,
and nice old ladies holding pitchers of lemonade
like on TV, my parents back together and loving
and caring for us kids, wanting us all to be one
happy and protected "one for all and all for one"
family.

I got kind of slaphappy, almost stoned by the
sun. One foot went in front of the other automatically, and I just floated along, alone, . . . in the
world, but not part of it . . . not even part of
myself. It was weird.

One car passed, slowed down, stared, then
speeded up again. I started bawling, moaning,
and groaning out loud. The car was filled with a
man and woman and kids. What if I had been their
kid? I had to be somebody's kid! I hadn't just
crawled out from under a rock on the desert. I had
to have a Mother and Father somewhere that con-
ceived me. In love or lust or something they still
joined their genes and chromosomes and cells and
stuff into some little magic seed mixture that made

me! Wasn't I anything? Anybody? Wasn't I important enough for one single person on earth to
care about? Could people just pass me up, stum-
bling along on a little-used road on the desert, and
watch me die without being at all responsible?
Weren't my parents responsible? Society? Anybody?

I began screaming, such loud and shrill and
inhuman sounds they hurt my ears, and I wanted
them to stop, but they wouldn't! They just kept
going on and on, bouncing over the hot sand and
over the dried-up little grubby shrubs, like one of
those crazy bouncing balls that you don't know in
which direction it will go, or when it will come
back to you.

Another car started toward me in the faraway
distance. It was smaller than an ant, then bigger
and bigger. I ran out in front of it, vowing I'd flag
it down or be run over. It would be better to die
under its wheels than to take maybe days having
the fact that nobody cared rubbed in.

The car, with a startled boggle-eyed older
woman and man, slowed down, almost stopped;
as I ran around the side to get in, it speeded off
the shoulder and down the highway in a black
stream of exhaust smoke. It had knocked me off
my feet.

I lay there groaning. Would they report the
incident to the police when they got to the nearest

121

phone, or would they live the rest of their lives with the fear that maybe they had killed me.

I wondered how I could kill myself and get it over with. I considered hitting myself over and over on the temple with a rock, but that would hurt too much. I wanted to die—not be hurt.

Maybe, as I walked along, I could find a broken bottle and cut my wrists. That gave me some encouragement, and I got up and began walking again. But there were no bottles, only rusty beer cans, lots and lots of rusty beer cans.

After what seemed like an eternity, I got desperate enough to try and cut my wrist with a rusty beer can, but it wasn't sharp enough to cause more than a trickle of blood, and besides, it hurt like hell trying to saw through the skin. I didn't know before that skin was so thick and hard to cut —almost like leather. Now I'd probably come down with tetanus or something, even if I didn't dehydrate on the desert. And I'd die a miserable death of suffering and torture and blood poisoning and stuff in some dirty little primitive old doctor's office, where neither the doctor nor the old nurse had read a medical magazine on updated things in the past forty years.

I was beginning to feel faint and I was glad! Maybe I'd pass out and the end would be kinder than I thought.

On the side of the road with a broken stick I

scratched the words, "I love you." I wanted to pass away loving somebody, anybody. NOT hating! The people who had left me hadn't hated me, they'd only been afraid and they had a right to be. Hitchhikers often mugged people and stole their cars and stuff and sometimes even killed people who were trying to help them. I walked a little farther and again I wrote. "Anybody, anywhere, I love you."

The stick was beginning to write wobbly, "Please, love me . . . please, somebody love me."

I remember thinking just before I blacked out that at least one person in the whole wide world *had* to love me . . .

I woke up in a grubby little office, just as I had imagined. Something hanging from a bottle at my side was dripping slowly into my arm. The doctor was old and wrinkled and stooped, and the nurse beside him seemed even older if possible, old and dried up as the desert. "Had a close call there, sonny," the doctor droned. "Sunstroke's one of the worst things we have in this area!"

"How did I get here?" I asked weakly, wanting to know desperately that someone had cared, yet afraid to know.

The nurse lifted up my head and put a straw into my mouth. "Take slow sips," she said in a voice as wizened as her face.

"How . . ." I started again.

The doctor answered, "A couple saw you weaving along the road and reported you to the sheriff."

My mouth and throat felt drier than ever. Obviously they hadn't mentioned that they had run me down. Oh, well . . . who'd believe me? Who'd want to know how brutally scared and hurt a kid can get?

Anyway, the doctor was kind. After I was feeling better, which didn't really take all that long, he took me to the bus station, which was part of the drugstore and restaurant, and bought me a bus ticket.

I was going home—home to my Mom! At first I was so elated it was like the neatest thing that had ever happened; then I began to worry about how she might feel. Sure she'd loved me when I was a little kid, bright and happy and like a toy or something she could manage. How would things be now that I was big and clumsy and unable to even understand myself? Did parents like kids to be pets or baby dolls, or little images of themselves, doing all the fun things they had done, or being all the things they'd wanted to be? It was scary . . . and so lonely. I looked around the bus at the other people on it. Two little old ladies in funny hats and wrinkled stockings and Dr. Scholl's shoes were laughing and giggling like two teenage girls, but everybody else seemed in

the pits, like me. All of us bleeding—inside lonely
. . . surrounded and suffocated by people, their
body odors, their breaths, even the heat from
their bodies; but we couldn't communicate,
couldn't relate, couldn't respond, couldn't care. It
was like we were not absolutely complete people,
like some special part that made us work together
or as one or something had been left out, or
placed imperfectly or something; so we couldn't
fulfill our function as human beings . . . at being
our brother's keeper . . . and all that.

How could we keep our brother when we
didn't even care about him? This sprawling, gagging, wrinkled, mottled bunch of semihuman beings on the bus obviously didn't care about themselves either, whether they lived or died, slept or
woke.

I had the deepest, most painful feeling inside.
We were malfunctioning. If we'd all been Hare
Krishnas, the bus would have been teeming with
laughter and love and concern and caring and
sharing, but that wasn't the answer either because
while it was superficially good, it could only eventually lead to stagnation for everybody.

I wished I had some Reds.

When I got off in Fort Worth, I was scared as if
I'd done something wrong. As I looked up Mom's
new phone under her new name, in her new

home with her new husband, I was so shaky my
fingers could hardly turn the pages. Man, what if
Mom didn't want me? What if I'd just be in the
way? What if George hated kids, especially teenagers? Everybody hated teenagers, everyone
knew that. I'd never met George, my new Father,
my other Father. He wasn't really my Father.
He'd been married before, but he'd never had
any kids. I guess he hadn't wanted any. Obviously
he hadn't wanted any. What ever made me think
he'd want me? I wasn't little bitty and cuddly. I
couldn't be rocked or played with or dangled on
his knee or any of the cute things parents want
from kids.

Oh, shit. Maybe it was all a big mistake, a big
shitty mistake! But it was too late to think about
that now. The first night out of New York some
slimy dudes had ripped off of me most of the
money I'd ripped off of my old man before I'd
split; and the only decent meal I'd had had been
at the crummy Hare Krishna place.

Life really was just one big manure pile after
another. I had meant to phone but decided it was
safer to just thumb to Mom's house. They
couldn't very well insult me when I turned up on
their doorstep. Or could they? What if George
was there alone? It wouldn't be hard for him to
tell me to get my ass someplace else. Oh, crum,
I wished I did have someplace else to go.

When Mom opened the door and saw me the
tears literally exploded out of her eyes and she
grabbed me so hard and hugged me so tight I
thought she was going to splinter my spine.

"Oh Mark, Mark, Mark, we've been so worried," she just kept telling me over and over.
Then she explained how Dad had called her the
first thing when Katie had showed him the note.
And how everybody had been frantic.

She had George get on the horn and call all the
relatives and tell them I was all right, and she
wouldn't even let me talk to Lee, my very favorite
forever friend, she was so busy asking me questions and telling me all about herself and her new
life.

It sounded great and I was happy for her.
George must be a pretty neat dude because he
made her feel special and competent and talented.
She even looked prettier and softer and she certainly acted more self-confident and capable.

As the evening went on, I noticed that George
never nitpicked at her like Dad had always done.
He thought she was neat, and I appreciated him
for that; in fact I loved and respected him from the
very beginning because of the way he treated her.
He didn't expect her to be his flunky and just
spend her life devoted to catering to him.

When I went to the bathroom, I peeked around

and noticed there was only one bedroom and their art studio. That would take care of me. "No room at the inn." But anyway, I could sleep for a few nights on the sofa in the living room. Not too long because sooner or later I'd be sure to throw off the harmony that Mom and George had and I didn't want to do that. Mom deserved all of the harmony she could get out of life. Everyone did. Besides, I'd never forget the black time when she was sick. I didn't want her to go through anything like that again, not if I could help it. And I certainly didn't intend in any way to be responsible for anything like that happening.

We talked almost the whole night long. George loved people and color and things. He said he'd never been much at making money, but by then I knew money wasn't the most important thing in the world. Lots of people worshiped money, but he didn't; he just considered it a nice thing to have, a necessity to buy physical things with.

I felt welcomed and relaxed from the very first with him, and was so glad for Mom that I tried hard not to think about myself and where I'd go from there.

On Sunday we all went down to Grandpa's and I couldn't believe the niceness of it. It was just like I'd never left, especially with Lee. He understood things without my ever having to tell him; I could see it in his eyes.

Grandma fixed all the special dishes I liked, and Aunt Jeannie and Sue brought some clothes of their kids I could wear. Man, it was neat.

During the whole weekend I didn't worry about what would come next; I just enjoyed. And Sunday when we all went to church together, even Mom and George, I really did feel like "my cup runneth over." My only sadness was that I missed Dad and I really, with all my heart and soul, missed Katie.

Late in the afternoon I went out into a little clump of trees and knelt down and thanked God for . . . well, just for everything. Man, God was so good to me. So tender and so kind and so watch-over-me.

Everyone just took it for granted that I'd cut out on Dad because I was lonesome for Mom, and they were all so good and kind and thoughtful that I couldn't tell them how it really was. No way could I tell any of them that. Living in little Happy Valley, they didn't need nightmares.

On Monday, Mom went by the school and picked up books for my grade. Everybody knew the school bit was no hassle to me. If they only knew about the other hassles inside my head.

I looked through all of the material they were using in their schools and was amazed at how different it was than ours.

Mom and George had an art showing set up in

some little mall in Abilene for two days, so I'd have the apartment by myself for the first day; then I'd take the bus up and we'd all come back together. It sounded kind of fun.

I watched TV and read till noon; then boredom began to set in. We'd all gotten up at 5:00 A.M. to get them off, so I'd already had a day, but I couldn't scrape myself off the ceiling so I could sleep.

It was when I was locking the apartment to go for a walk that I noticed Mom's car keys on the ring. Man, that's what I'd do, take her little Rabbit out for a few hops, just cruise around. I'd never driven before, but any kid with his head out of his butt had watched and hoped and pretended often enough.

It wasn't really any problem. A few jerky starts and motor killings and I was cruising like I'd been driving forever.

At first I kind of stayed to the back streets and drove like the little old lady in tennis shoes you hear about; then I started revving it up.

I picked up one kid who obviously was thumbing a ride to school from the books under his arms and took him there, just showing off.

I had lunch at a drive-in and flirted with the waitress and made a date with her for the weekend. I probably wouldn't even be here, and I certainly wouldn't have a car. But it made me feel like a big shot laying it on about how my old man had given me the Rabbit for my birthday. When she picked up my tray, I left her the biggest tip I'd ever given. And she gave me a carrot to feed my car!

Man, it was exhilarating! Cruising up and down the streets, trying to take off before anyone else at the stop signs, just generally playing "BMIT." About five o'clock, when I'd decided I better get home 'cause Mom might call, I saw a little blond angel-looking type kid thumbing on the opposite side of the street. I whipped around and skidded up to him, "Where ya going, sport?" I asked as he climbed in. I wanted to really impress him with my smooth. He was about Katie's age, ten maybe eleven. In fact, he even reminded me of her in a lot of ways, big innocent blue eyes, fragile looking and vulnerable.

"Just going," he said, seeming kind of uptight.

Suddenly, a protective father figure kind of lecturing started pouring out of me. I couldn't stop it. I offered to take him home, begged to take him home.

He seemed even more nervous. I offered to take him to a hamburger stand. He shook his head, and I could see big tears trying to squeeze out of his eyes.

"Then come to my apartment for awhile," I offered.

He grinned, a salty, wet little grimace. "Man, we'll get it on as many times as you want and any way you want for . . ." he hesitated,". . . twenty dollars."

I couldn't believe my ears, my mouth hung down to my chest.

"Ten dollars?" he pleaded.

"Are you saying what I think you're saying, kid?" I asked, still not able to accept it.

"Any way you want it, big buddie," he answered, trying to keep his voice from shaking.

I gagged.

"You up, me up, or razzle-dazzle," he whispered.

I didn't even know what he was talking about.

"Please," he whimpered, "can't you see I'm hurting. Pay me first and let me pick up my stuff and I'll give you a job you'll never forget."

I groaned. "Let me take you to a drug clinic or a church or someplace for help," I pleaded. "They can help you get off the stuff." I sniffed back my own hot tears. "Honest, they can. I'll stay with you till you're safe, I promise."

He put his hand out to open the car door. I reached out and grabbed him back. I wouldn't have him on the street. A male whore at ten, maybe eleven at the most, selling himself for junk, for . . . I almost hit a car as I tried to hang on to him in the traffic, but he slipped away. Off into the dark, clutching shadows that would swallow him up and hide him till he found some dirty deviate who'd take a little kid and . . .

I wanted to throw up and drove around and around the area until the gas indicator showed almost empty. O God, what a way to live.

I called the police station when I got home, but the guy in the juvenile division didn't seem too shocked or concerned. Didn't even think there was anything they could do, but he'd have the patrol car in the area keep their eyes open for a little blond boy about ten or eleven on the streets soliciting. He hung up in midsentence. While he'd been talking to me, he was talking to some other guy in the background about basketball tickets.

I put Mom's car back in the garage and decided I'd go back to Dad's right away. O dear God, I was so depressed. I knew how Mom had felt during her bad time. Life really wasn't worth living. It was filled up and overflowing with ugliness and loneliness. The loneliness was almost more than I could bear. At least with Dad Katie was always there even when he wasn't. I needed her. I needed him. I needed someone.

Desperate, I called Lee long distance, but he and his Dad were out on a Red Cross drive. That made me even more lonely.

The apartment floors creaked when I walked on

them. Everything smelled of oil paints and turpentine and stuff. The sofa was lumpy and cold. There was only health food, no junk stuff, in the refrigerator. And it was quiet, quiet—eerie quiet.

I went in Mom's closet and sat in the corner on her shoes. When I shut the door it smelled like her, soft and warm and sweet. I curled up tighter and slept there all night.

Back in New York everything was the same, school during the day, TV at night. Dad told me that Elisha had moved to the San Francisco office and had leased her apartment. That really took a load off me. With her around I had felt like an animal in the jungle—the sophisticated huntress with traps in every conceivable place, nets hanging in the elevator, trapdoors in the laundry room . . . Oh, shit, I was so paranoid it was pitiful.

Katie and I had started doing our gym clothes and stuff we had to do together. I had told her I didn't like the looks and actions of the assistant janitor in the building, and the poor little innocent slob believed me. What would she ever have thought if she had known I was only trying to protect myself? But maybe I was trying to protect her, too. If there were weirdie women in the building, there were probably plenty of weirdo men, too. Yeah, she needed all the protection she could get. Crap, some nights I'd lie awake and wonder if kids all over the world were preyed on like the kids in America? What had happened to society, where, instead of it protecting innocent little ones, they had become the quarry, the victims? I'd heard that baby prostitutes were the rage; did that include little boys, too? Oh, man, what a despicable evil world! I wished I could get that little blond boy out of my mind, but I couldn't. Would I ever be able to, even when I had children of my own? Shit, doping was one thing, but its by-products were . . . I had to get up and start nipping on Dad's booze. Was I too sensitive? Was I too concerned and alarmed? Should I try harder to detach myself and try to pretend that these things didn't exist—like most adults do? Maybe they did it out of sheer self-preservation, to save their sanity, their lives. Were the pressures of society part of the reason Mom had tried to end it all? In a way I wished everybody could end it all. *That* was morbid! I had to pull myself out of it.

I'd only been gone thirteen days, but it seemed like years. Sandy was back doping again. She maintained really well and nobody ever guessed or maybe cared how much she was using, but I worried. I knew she was getting loaded with a pretty big habit. Where was she getting the bread? We tried to be friends, really tried, but it just didn't work any more. It was too tough on me trying to carry her problems along with those of my own, and besides you can't help someone who doesn't want help. I tried to get her to go talk to some church person somewhere like we used to talk about doing. Someone who could help her get herself together, but she said that didn't sound or feel "right" any more.

Sandy was a special neat kid, and I hated to see her go down the drain, but there didn't seem to be much I could do except just stand around and watch her. Often I wondered if the teachers in school didn't know how continually spaced out she was, or didn't they care? When kids used downers, they sat back in their own groovy little world and didn't bother anybody. In fact I'd always suspected that most teachers would like passing out Reds every morning and after every lunch period just to make their jobs easier. But Sandy was on some kind of flippers. Man, she was running up and down the halls laughing and hugging and joking and revving like I always wanted to do. But uppers didn't turn me on like that; they splattered me all over the walls.

Man, did parents and teachers really even suspect what went on behind their backs and often right in front of their eyes? And the local and school narcs? Man, sometimes it seemed they were only after the pushers and didn't give a shit about the everyday using, everyday growing, feeding their habit users and losers.

The whole thing was one big long—from 9:00 A.M. to 3:30 P.M.—bummer.

I read about some schools around the country that allow high school and even junior high kids to take college classes if they're mentally up to it, and I could hardly wait to go see my counselors and make arrangements to do it. It would be no sweat at all because school had always been the biggest of easy bores in the world to me. Classes were almost like baby-sitting sessions, teachers so busy keeping order, or trying to keep kids from killing each other and messing up the teachers themselves, that all the material that was taught through the whole semester a good student could get in about a week. And the kids who couldn't get it, or who were behind, just got ignored and never did have a chance to see how the puzzle worked.

It was like us kids who had brains had to be ashamed of them, and kids who had physical prowess wouldn't share if their lives depended on it. I know that because a few weeks before I'd thought Luke Brown was the neatest physical thing that had ever been born. Man, he was just as good in basketball as he was in football and baseball. I wanted so much to share just one little thread of his power and glory that one time when

I met him at the drugstore, I offered to tutor him three hours scholastically for every hour that he'd tutor me in sports. You know what the a-hole did? He punched me in the nose, and within days it was all around school what a creep I was, trying to make a lily-liver out of the school hero. Yeah, the illiterate school hero, who couldn't even read his assignments in class, say nothing about doing them. How come everybody worshiped him? He'd wind up a dumb dock worker just like his old man, and nobody would give a damn, they just wanted to milk him for all the publicity and school drawing power he had for the moment. Nobody cared, even the teachers, that he couldn't read or even add up the numbers on his lunch ticket. Crap, what a crappy system.

Anyway, the incident made me a leper at school, to be stoned, laughed at, a joked-about sissy. In fact the stories grew till I was painted to be a fluffy queer trying to make it with all the big boys on the teams. Nobody cared that in the long-range program it was the brains that kept the world progressing. They just cared for the screwed-up, going nowhere, leading nowhere, now.

About my taking some college classes or even going to college as a full-time student, the vice-principal said he'd look into it, the counselor said she'd take it up with her committee, my teachers just smiled and wished that I, along with all the other students in their classes, would just disappear. They really didn't give one damn or another how we did it.

Days passed and I bugged them; more time passed and they just got upset when they saw me coming. At the end of three weeks they were all openly hostile toward me, like I was asking some big personal favor that was far beyond their means.

I talked to Dad and he said he'd check into it when he had time. Which meant next never day.

It was really getting to me, the hassling at school about my being an overt fairy fingers. Sandy didn't help much detailing our relationship together and even coloring up some . . . a whole lot in fact!

Talk about friends. No wonder kids aren't often associated with "friends" any more. It's always "peers," yeah, peers, someone your own age but not necessarily close to you. Nobody's close to anybody unless you're drawn together in a unit to tear somebody else down.

Man, it kept getting grosser and grosser. Somebody sprayed purple paint on my leather jacket, and guys kept handing me love notes they had obviously cooked up together, filthy degenerate things that left me literally emotionally drained.

In gym, the guys were always trying to get me

in the showers, and I couldn't get down any crowded hall without having at least one bully tweak my . . . ah . . . well . . .

I began cutting more and more classes and I went back to Reds. Suicide was beginning to seem more and more like the only way out. Man, life was a crapper.

I wished I had some place to go so I could think and try and get the pieces put together. I felt like Humpty Dumpty, but no one was trying with me like they did with him. They just seemed to be kicking my pieces farther and farther away from me.

Maybe I was going crazy. I wanted to be alone . . . I had to be alone . . . And then I was. And *it* wasn't what I wanted either.

Dad had gone off on some business weekend, and Katie was staying with a friend. I had the whole house to myself. For one time it was quiet —what I'd always wanted a few minutes of! But there's something sinister and lonely about quiet . . . lonely and colorless. It made me think about death even more. Why wouldn't anybody accept that death existed. They wouldn't talk about it or even say it. "Death . . . death . . . death." I started to say aloud to myself, "die . . . die . . . die . . . die . . . die."

I wondered if I had ever heard those words used before. At funerals they always said, like we were all cultists with the greatest of taboos upon death, that Uncle John Doe or whoever had "passed away" or "passed on" or "taken his last trip" or "been given the last rites," or whatever.

And when the goldfish or the bird or the turtle died, they always skirted the word and "replaced it," and stuff. I wanted to *talk* about life and death, and where we came from, and what we were doing here, and where were we going and was it all the hell worth it.

I thought that's what's partly wrong with this screwed-up society. Everybody's ideas and values are up their asses. It seems like they're all struggling to survive against all the odds in the universe. And why? Kids mostly have no hope. It's just not worth the hassle. What's the reward? Even a donkey sees a carrot at the end of a stick. Why is life better than death, especially when apparently no one even knows what death is, or wants to talk about it? Actually it's kind of funny, but it's hard to think and talk about suicide when you're feeling pretty good, but man, when you're down, you're really down. Food doesn't taste like anything edible—kind of like gray ground-up cotton, and colors mostly fade into blacks and grays.

I remembered once thinking how everything had lost its flavor and color and how even music, which I loved, seemed just kind of a noisy distraction or something.

I guess really no one can understand except someone who has had those lonely, lost feelings. Everything seems so useless . . . You can't relate and you just keep sinking deeper and deeper into this grayed kind of protoplasmic nothingness.

When I'd tried to talk to Dad or my school counselor, they were both bummers. The horror of people telling you to "shape up" and "look up" is almost sadistically cruel, like beating an innocent dog just because he has been run over. That's how I felt lots of times, that I'm maimed and bleeding in an inside, quiet, unbelonging way, and that people, instead of tending to my wounds, just gouged at them. I didn't want to be depressed. God in heaven knows I didn't want to be depressed! I wasn't a sadistic weirdo who runs out and looks for hurts; in fact I always tried to run away from quarrels and fights and stuff, but you can't run away from depression, honestly you can't! No matter where you go, it follows right after you like a nightmare, getting closer and closer and more and more frightening: And people, no matter who they are, telling you to "keep smiling" and all that bull; they just don't know what it's all about. It's like telling you when you've got a broken leg or appendicitis that if you'll just think about something else, it will go away. It won't! I've tried!

In the library once I found a booklet that said some kinds of depression are chemical, so I begged Dad to let me go to a doctor, but that just seemed kind of dumb to him. I wasn't limping or fainting or running a fever, or had a lump or a sore that wouldn't heal or something serious like that. Depression only makes you bleed on the inside where it won't show. Maybe that's a good thing because if half the teenagers in the country were bleeding externally, it would be a pretty slippery-red-gory-bloody world. I wondered would anybody care then and take us seriously?

As I was thinking about how kids want to die and adults want to survive, it was like a big black cloud unfolded upon me from all four corners of my room. It covered me and smothered me. Frankly, it scared the hell out of me! I thought that's what it was: death. And I struggled like hell to get out of it. I prayed and fought and repented. If that's what death was, I didn't want any part of it. No wonder adults couldn't and wouldn't face it.

Then morning sunlight started streaming through my window and the blackness went away. It was really funny, but I knew that death wasn't like the blackness at all. It was more like the sunshine and becoming part of the brightness and light. Life was the blackness, like what people

really think death is, and death is going into another realm of light and beauty without the problems and pressures.

I knew adults would think I was psycho, but I
didn't give a damn what adults thought any more.
They certainly didn't have the answers.

I tried to talk to a minister once about suicide
and death, but he just shook his head and retreated; he couldn't even say the word. And he
kept saying over and over, "May God forgive
you," how to take life was murder, and I'd be like
the most evil murderer in the world. I couldn't
stand it. I felt degenerate and forever condemned
to the eternal burnings of hell for even having
thought about it. But that didn't stop me from
thinking about it every time the pressure got
more than I could stand.

I knew I needed help, but I didn't know how
to get it. I was rejected by everything and everyone. If only someone would listen and respond,
not just the minister's "Don't worry, it's all right"
baloney.

One day Carlos, the janitor in our building, said
I looked sad, and I could have hugged him. Everyone else called me "negative" and "dull." It was
wonderful to have someone recognize that I was
depressed. We sat for hours on the basement
steps, then down in his apartment talking about it.
He told me how for years he had taken Valium

and stuff to keep "upped" enough to even exist. And that coping wasn't so bad if you had a little something to help you do it. He said once he had been sent to a psycho ward because he had jumped through a plate glass window hoping to bleed to death. Isn't that sadistic that they send people who are so depressed that they want to kill themselves to a place with crazy people? Anyway, he said there were lots of kids there, more kids than grown-ups by far.

He got out his mental health pamphlets, and I can remember like they are red neon words and figures before me, that almost all young people have destructive thoughts, that suicides among the young and very young have gone up over 200 percent in the last ten years. And that suicide is still growing among teenagers, and there are over 400,000 attempts every year. And that one half of all kids have suicide thoughts often, and 10 percent of those who try eventually make it. This one book said most attempts are cries for help, or to get attention, but I didn't really think that was what was wrong with me. I just thought I was weak and life was too heavy for me, but I didn't know . . . these people that make surveys ought to know what they're talking about, but . . . well . . . I didn't think I was trying to get attention, but I presume I was crying for . . . some kind of understanding . . . or caring . . .

I couldn't stand it alone, and no one seemed to relate to me. I talked to Sandy about my feelings, and how I'd tried to kill myself, and she just told all the kids at school, and they, on top of everything else, teased me and laughed at me and suggested things for me to do like put a plastic bag over my head and stick my head in the toilet and drown.

All that kind of stuff made me even more alone. I knew I wasn't the only one who had thought that way, I'd heard Sandy and Ted and a million others all say they wanted to kill themselves, but in a group they got strength for themselves by cutting me.

Carlos became the only one I could trust, the only one who understood. And gradually we got into a sexual relationship. I only felt secure and cared for when I was with him. It didn't matter about his filthy room, or the fact that he never bathed, or any of the physical things, or that the whole setup repulsed me. I needed someone, and he was all I could find.

When Carlos just cut out one night, I began to plan my funeral. This time I really would die. People would weep and mourn for me. They'd come to the mortuary and tell about what a neat person I'd been, how beautiful and kind and good. How helpful and thoughtful. And the teachers would come and say how good I'd been in school and how much they had loved me and loved helping me, and the kids would lie, too. The more I lived in my fantasy the more glorious it became and I put off killing myself just because the thoughts of it were so wonderful. At last I'd be someone important! Clean and beautiful and white lying in that open casket. It would be greater even than the party at Uncle Marco's restaurant, but this time, instead of laughing and dancing and singing, there would be kind things said and tears. After awhile, after many ups and downs in my plans, I began to feel better. Then I was ashamed. Could God ever forgive me for my suicidal thoughts? Would He? Could I ever forgive myself?

The guilties took over. I guess nothing can be worse than the guilties, unless maybe it's a case of the terminal guilties, which is what I hoped I had . . . but I hoped I didn't have, too.

A girl in our building committed suicide, and Dad raved about how disgusting it was and how she had disgraced her family. I was glad I hadn't killed myself. I didn't want to hurt any of my relatives. They were nice. They were kind. They were wonderful. They just didn't understand how down a person can get.

Things started getting better at school. Joanie and I became friends. It's a great feeling having a friend, someone who cares about you, and who you can talk to. She was black, so that made it a little difficult for my Dad, a dyed-in-the-wool Texan, but at sixteen I guessed I could at least pick out my own friends.

We spent a lot of time at Joanie's place. It was quiet there because she was the youngest one, and her Mom worked. One day I got up guts enough to tell her about my suicide feelings. She said she had had them too, and we fell into each other's arms and cried. It really was secure to finally have someone who understood and who wasn't just using me.

It's funny how, when you're happy, everything is so much easier. Me and Joanie discussed things for hours—school, hopes for the future, coping at home, everything, boy-girl relationships, boy-boy relationships, girl-girl relationships, black-white relationships. It was the best part of my life, except when I was real little. It was like the weather had changed from winter to summer. I was glad to be alive. The feelings were too wonderful to contain some days. I'd go to Central Park and not be able to believe the wonder of nature and God and mankind and everything. I wanted to yell and paint the whole world sunshine yellow, so that even when the clouds came, they would have to reflect its glow.

Then Joanie fell in love with Joe, her friend who had been in the service. For a while I was glad for her and glad for him, too. They were both special neat people and both black, which would lessen the hassle. But each day I could feel the sunshine drain out of myself. I fought to keep it from going. I didn't want to be lonely and rejected again. I prayed harder than I had ever prayed before and I went to my Grandparents' church and every other church in the area. But nothing helped. I could feel myself losing the battle with depression. I began to have day and nightmares of mental hospitals and things disgusting like Carlos had told me about. I knew he hadn't lied. Both television and newspapers told about people sent to mental hospitals because they had tried to end it all. I began writing poems about death, beautiful poems about the escapeful restfulness of it and the busy, pressured awfulness of life.

I'm making it sound like I was all the time morbid, and I wasn't; there were probably more good times than there were bad, more up times than there were down times. Sometimes it even seemed dumb that I ever considered death over life, especially since I couldn't talk about it to anyone. Once in the library, or in an article in a magazine, or newspaper or something I read again that one half of the teenage population polled by a big group, had considered suicide. I found it amazing and alarming that every other person I met or passed in the halls had at one time or another, to one degree or another, felt like I have; rejected, unhappy, alone, unworthy, desperate. I remember taking an oath that I would be kind and more friendly and considerate of everyone I knew or met in case I might be the one bright thread that would keep them from complete loneliness, that utter loneliness that I guess no adult ever really feels. Maybe it's a new thing with our generation; maybe we've just been squeezed out of the meaning and importance of life by birthrate zero and ecology and women's lib and all that kind of stuff.

O dear God, there really is something wrong with me. I need help. I'm scared to death I'll try to commit suicide and botch it and be sent to a mental hospital and locked inside bars and grilles and stuff. I couldn't stand that! I'm terrified of mental hospitals and what goes on there, and I'm terrified that I'll disgrace and humiliate and embarrass my family. I can't relate to them, but I don't want to hurt them. They want so much of me . . . the whole world does, and I can't produce . . . or maybe I just expect too much of myself. I wish I knew what was normal. I wish we had classes where people wouldn't be afraid to discuss subjects like that and death. It's almost a joke to try and talk to somebody about it as it is. I can just see myself going up to anyone, just plain anyone, and saying, "I want to talk about death. What's so bad about it? What's so good about it? Why can't people discuss it? Why does everybody try to ignore it and pretend it doesn't exist? Everybody's someday going to have to experience it, aren't they? It isn't like death is something unusual or unique or that happens to only a few."

I read once somewhere that all failure people have one thing in common, a poor self-image; and I guess that's true because everybody I've ever known, no matter how great they were, always had some part of them that felt insecure and not quite good enough, or strong enough, or something. Us real failure people have a whole lot of the same!

Often I wonder if you outgrow those feelings. I keep telling myself people do because adults all seem to feel all right about themselves, but maybe that's because they've got kids to lord it over.

But, anyway, that part is true about a low self-image making you feel like a failure and wanting to just give up and get it over with. Then why don't people build kids up? Why are they always tearing us down? "Your hair is too long." "Your pants are too tight." "You're lazy." "You're so damned slow and procrastinating about everything." And the teachers and school officials want us to do everything for them, but they won't do anything for us like finding out about my taking college classes. I passed all the entrance requirements I wrote for. Sometimes it seems like all of life is out to get you or pressure or mold you into something that isn't even you. It's like a tight trap getting tighter and heavier.

After Joanie and I broke up, I called Mom and made a desperate attempt to talk to her about it, but she just laughed and called the experience "puppy love" and said I'd get over it in a while, that it wasn't all that important. I tried to talk to Dad and Katie and Ted and everybody else I knew, but they just fluffed it off, "Joanie isn't the only fish in the sea."

Nobody seemed to sense how deeply hurt I was, how deeply and endlessly depressed. I went to bed for three days, literally unable to function. Dad said I had the flu again and told Katie to stay away from me. I remember thinking I was more alone than I had ever been in my whole life.

Dad had an office party at the apartment. I could hear the laughing, and the talking, and the singing, and the quarreling and fighting, but I wasn't part of it . . . I was alone . . . desperately, frighteningly . . . a failure, alone. There in the very midst of the wildest kind of belonging and relating . . . I was alone . . . completely alone . . . I didn't belong . . . I didn't relate . . . It was like I was dead already and just a bodiless invisible spirit in the midst of all the physicalness.

That probably doesn't make any sense at all. Someone being their very loneliest in the middle of a big crowd, but that's the way it is sometimes. Nothing can be more lonely than a crowd. Being in a big tangle of people being pushed and shoved and crunched and thinking, these people are pushing and shoving me, touching me and breathing on me, but they don't know me, they don't care about me. I could fall down, and they could walk on me and squash me till my guts smashed out, and my eyes popped loose, and my blood sloshed up on their shoes and legs, and they would only be annoyed that I was getting them red and bloody and oozy, that maybe my guts were slippery. See, I really am morbid.

I tried to explain to Dad, but he couldn't see my side, couldn't feel my feelings, my sorrow, my despair. When I told him I'd maybe commit suicide, he laughed at me and called me melodramatic.

I planned it so it would seem like an accident. To my family and relatives, suicide was self-murder, which would forever blacken their family name. I'd have to be very careful. I began reading the papers about accidents. Which one could I set up for myself?

I had to cross a busy intersection on my way to school. I'd wait at the bus stop for a big fast truck and run out in front of it.

As I made my plans, Dad and Katie were pleased with my change in attitude, that I seemed to be getting back more into the mainstream of life. I was kinder and more considerate to them. I tried to get things in order at school and with my friends. I wanted to make it as easy on everybody as possible. Even my gym teacher commented one day about how much better I was doing. He just didn't know that it was the planned lull before the storm. But when I got it all ready, I had myself so psyched up I didn't need it. I just made a half-hearted attempt. Isn't that weird? Actually I guess all of life is pretty weird when you try to put the pieces together, and sometimes can't.

Well, anyway, I'm feeling pretty "with it" right now and of course I'm hoping I can keep it this way, but I just seem to be one of those kids that can't stand pressure. But then I guess that doesn't make me so awfully different because apparently, according to statistics, every other second kid can't either. I wonder if all their parents and the rest of the adults around them are as unsuspecting as those around me, or as apathetic.

One thing for sure, my Mom and Dad and the rest of the people I know would never dream that I would do such a thing as suicide, and the religious people take it so lightly I don't know if they don't know or don't care. They're the only ones I've ever used the word around. I mean adults.

I've talked to a lot of kids, but they're all as screwed-up as I am. Death . . . death . . . death . . . die . . . die . . . die. It's kind of neat being able to say the words aloud without feeling like a creep. The only thing I can't understand and don't like to think about is being buried in the cold, black, dark ground. I know . . . I don't care what other people think . . . that that's just a person's body in the casket . . . and that their spirit has gone back to heaven where it's quiet and peaceful and caring, but it's still kind of creepy. I try to tell myself that the body is just like an old suit, that it's just a physical covering for the spirit, but it seems so intimate and personal. I want it, too, and I want to believe that after the resurrection my body and spirit will be rejoined again. That makes sense to me and it feels sound, and I really don't want to commit suicide. But I don't know . . . sometimes life gets so heavy and problems get so strangling. Oh, I do hope I can make it. I want to get married and have a couple of little kids and make them feel loved and needed and important, so they won't have to go through all the pit stuff I've felt. I want to talk to them and relate to them and let them know they are important and needed and that I love them.

But about suicide, if someone says they're going to do it, they most likely are, at least if they can get their hands on something to do it with that very moment. When I really tried, it was mostly, I guess, because there was something at hand to try with. Like the time I tried it with pills, I just cleaned out the medicine cabinet and whatever it was that I found, I swallowed. And when I tried with the gas stove, it didn't work because Katie came home, but I think I might have if she hadn't. And the time with booze it was just there. I think real attempts are impulsive because when I had time to really plan, I never did. If someone just knew and cared enough to protect us from ourselves for a couple of hours, or a couple of weeks, or whatever, I think most kids would make it through the dark lonely valleys in their lives.

It's no good for parents to say, like mine did, "Oh come on, snap out of it," "Start smiling," "Start looking at the good side," and all that stuff because you really can't control it. Honest you can't! At least I couldn't and I think I'm average and normal . . . but then again maybe I'm not; maybe I'm just a suicidal been-nowhere going-nowhere crazy that really ought to be locked up; but I hope not. Honest to God I hope not.

Life really is strange. I wonder if it's just in our American culture that there seem to be the constant battles going on. Not people working together, or even trying to work together, but the dumb kids hating and resenting the smart kids, the big jocks making swipes at the not-so-coordinated, not-so-popular kids, and the . . . oh, hell, the whole school ground, maybe the whole world is like one giant battlefield. Whatever happened to "brotherly love," "love thy neighbor as thyself"?

I want to love people. I want them to love and respect me. I wonder if deep down inside everyone else feels the same way . . . afraid and hurt . . . and lonely.

I wonder if I'll ever find the right way to follow, or if there is a right way.

I've just finished reading about National Family Week, and, man, that seems like the answer if people would work at it. But they don't. President Ford said in 1976, "It is in our families that we learn, develop and practice those attitudes and concepts of right and wrong, of fairness, of charity, and love of country. Neither schools nor the institutions of government can ever replace the American family in the development of responsible and caring individuals.

"The success of our American experiment in self-government depends upon the unique character of the American spirit—a spirit that is nurtured, taught by example, and lived by experience within the vital framework of the American family.

"It is within the family circle that each child learns the most important of life's lessons: from parents, love and respect; from grandparents, and other older relatives, wisdom and tolerance. These family experiences nurture our sense of community with others.

"In deprivation and abundance, in turmoil and tranquility, Americans have reached out for their destiny from this constant sanctuary of life."

Man, that sounds great, but it's just so much more shit, too. Everybody knows that there are more kids by far today from broken homes than there are from complete ones. It's no longer a "family" thing in parents' lives, it's a "me" thing. Everybody thinking only about their own libido and their own successes and fulfillments. To hell with everybody and anybody else that might get in their way, including their kids. O dear God, I wish I had people I love and could trust here, like Lee and Tim and Todd.

Now I'm beginning to sound like those crazy Hare Krishna slobs I met in New Mexico. But maybe *they're right!* Maybe they really do have the answers, and I was, just like what I'm condemning adults for, too engrossed in their orange robes and their cuckoo haircuts to see what they are really all about deep down inside. I wasn't really listening, not really wanting to hear when I talked to them. Actually I, like I guess everybody else at first, was trying to trip up their concepts, trying to belittle or confuse their thinking, not willing to accept it if it doesn't fit in exactly with my own. Man, I'm just as much of a screwed-up pooper as all the people I've been so down on. But things are going better, and next year I'll be going to a new school and I'm going to try harder to conform there and be likeable. And I guess it really is true that you find what you're looking for in life, so I'm going to try harder to look for the good stuff, and forget the yuck that's gone behind. Good luck to me, hey?

MILLIE
the homosexual alternative

O.K., I'll start back as far as I can remember. I guess I was three or four maybe, and we were a nice family. Mama and Daddy played games with me and took me to the zoo and stuff. For summers Grandma and Grandpa Ivy came from Nebraska, and I remember the presents were higher than me almost.

I guess the bad stuff all started happening when I was about, oh, maybe seven or so. No, I guess I was eight because I remember I was in the third grade. Well, anyways I was in the third grade when my parents got their divorce. I remember them sitting and talking and talking to me about it, and how they were just thinking of me and all crapola stuff like that. Miss Peterson was my teacher, and she kept asking me was I sick because I was all the time sad and crying and stuff. I guess at that point she really was the only one thinking about me because, while Mama and Daddy were insisting they were only trying to do what was best for me, they wouldn't even listen to how I felt about having my whole family and my whole life torn up in front of my very eyes.

I remember lying in bed and thinking and crying and coming to the conclusion it must all be my fault because they kept saying everything they were doing was for me. I had nightmares and wet the bed. O dear God, what had I done wrong to make them hate each other and me enough to want to break up our family? To have Daddy move to another town, and Mom put our beautiful house up for sale? Our beautiful, nice house with the skinny winding stairs and the big fireplace in the family room, which I loved and the kitchen that baked cookies and spaghetti and stuff, which I loved. I used to call it "pasgetti." And they used to think it was funny when I slurped the long, slippery, stringy ends in like a vacuum. Oh, we laughed and laughed so much. Before we all started crying. I guess they cried, but maybe not. It's hard to know about what goes on in parents' heads. Sometimes I think it's their own little worlds in there and nobody else can get through, not even their children. With kids it's different; our worlds are kind of put together by pieces of other people's worlds. It's kind of like we're born with perfectly good, but blank computers, and everything we hear and see and come in contact with computes into patterns which, for good or bad, become us. Oh, that's ridiculous because people are what they want to be. I dunno. . . . I guess I better get back to what I was telling.

Well, after the divorce Dad just sort of cut us out of his life, both Mom and me. Oh, I went to stay with him at summertimes, but it wasn't the same.

I remember the day of the divorce. I guess I had thought it really wouldn't happen if I willed it hard enough not to, but it did.

Mom came home all beautiful and dry-eyed, joking with her friend May and telling me how she and Dad both still loved me.

Man, like now I can just see myself slipping off to my room, a human animal to hurt by myself, while Mom and May sat in the living room escaping with liquor. I didn't know about that then, or believe me, I'd have been right there beside them with the bottle. I wish I had a drink, or an upper, or a downer or something right now because it still hurts when I think about it like I'm being cut open all over again.

Oh, something else . . . when I heard Mama and her girlfriend out there laughing after they'd gotten high enough, I couldn't stand it. I really couldn't stand it! My head hurt, and I cried till there literally weren't any tears left in my whole body. I remember wondering how I could still be sobbing and sniffing and crying dryness. Our family, our nice warm protected family, was all broken up and Mama was laughing. I wondered if Daddy was off in a bar or someplace laughing, too. Both of them living it up while our whole world had been smashed to pieces. No family, no Mother, no Father. We were all broken up, not important to anything or anybody—pieces of nothing.

I cry even now when I remember taking my cherished doll collection and one by one smashing and cutting them into little pieces, like I felt I was. I wanted them, my family, to feel like I felt, wanted them to be part of the nothing, the not belonging world I had been thrust into.

Well, anyway I got over that. I visited Dad in the summers and once in a while on a holiday vacation. He always told me what a wonderful Mother I had, and she gave me the same old line about him. But I knew they were both lying. If they had been so great, they would have stayed together. I guess I blamed him most because he was the one who talked to me about the divorce first, and he was the one who finally left.

I can't remember much about the next few years but that I was alone a lot and it was lonely.

Somehow voices on radio and television and stuff just aren't the same as real people talking, even yelling and arguing.

To get on, Mama started going with different guys, but none of them ever paid much attention to me. Anyway, by that time I knew why they were paying attention to her. Once one of them, when he was a little stoned, even pulled up my dress and put his hands under *my* pants.

At about twelve years old I remember talking to Mama about things like that, wanting her to tell me to be clean and pure, but she just told me I didn't understand and tried to explain about "meaningful relationships."

Meaningful relationships, shit! Oh, crap, now I'm being mean and vindictive. She really was a good Mother in her own way, and I think she had only, maybe four or five boyfriends. I made her sound like she was humping every jock on the street, and it wasn't anything like that; it was just that the guys were so . . . so gross. I guess actually they weren't even that. Mac was a doctor whose wife had died, and Mama went with him for a long time; and then David, who ran a big restaurant chain; and Bruce, who was a radio disc jockey and . . . I don't even like to talk about Jake. He's the one who tried to roll me, and he beat up on Mom once. Man, that was awful, me coming in and finding him beating up on her.

I wanted to kill him, and when she sobered up a bit she wanted to kill him, too. I sat there rocking her in my arms like she was the kid, and she told me what rotten bloody bastards men really are, even my Dad, a bloody bastard pit.

It was never the same again after that, with any of us. And the more I thought about the male species, the more I knew Mom was right. They were rotten, brutal sons of bitches all after one thing, and out to get it in any way possible. Crap, by then I guess I was thirteen . . . yes, I was, because I had just started junior high, and the jocks were always pinching bottoms in the halls or trying to titty twist, which wasn't all that easy with me because there wasn't much there. Anyways, they were just a bunch of junior bastards. Not all of them because I did have some good friends in the school band, but mostly boys were just "yuck"!

After Christmastime when I was feeling about my loneliest and forsaken, Mrs. Stephens, my typing teacher, asked me to stay after school and help her do some typing for the school yearbook. That really made me happy. It was nice feeling like somebody needed me. Sometimes we worked late, and she took me out to dinner. One Saturday we even went skiing. I remember it was so much fun. It was the first time I had laughed and felt warm and important to an adult in so long it was almost like starting my computers all over again.

Mrs. Stephens was just getting a divorce, but she was not like Mom; she seemed lonely and vulnerable. It made me feel good that I could warm up her world a little the way she was warming up mine. Sometimes we'd sit in her apartment at nights, and she'd scratch my back and brush my hair. It made me feel very little, and very feminine and very important. It was nice being important to somebody, being needed, being wanted, giving joy.

After about two weeks, Mrs. Stephens (by now I was calling her Faye when we were alone) warned me that we'd have to play it a little cool at school or everyone would think I was the "teacher's pet." Then she hugged and kissed me lightly and told me I really was. I remember the joy that brought me. I was Mrs. Stephens' pet. Wow! She was the favorite teacher at our junior high school. I wanted to scream out as I walked up and down the halls that I was "her pet," her special friend, that she loved me! She'd told me so. All her other students would be so jealous! So jealous they wouldn't be able to stand it, I thought.

I was beginning to spend almost as much time at Mrs. Stephens'—Faye's—as I was at home. I'd help her in her office from about three-thirty, when I got out, till about four or four-thirty, when she was through with all her stuff; then I'd walk, and she'd drive over to her place so people wouldn't see us together. I had a key to the apartment and sometimes I'd even sneak over a little early and do little things for her, things that made me scream like a banshee when Mom made me do them at home, but things were fun to do for Faye.

I'd always make it home just in time for dinner, and I'd started telling Mom I was at the library or a friend's house because Faye said Mom might be jealous of the time I spent with her. I felt that was dumb, but anything Faye said was all right with me. At that point I felt she cared about me, that she was always and only interested in what was best for me, what would make me happy, what would make me a better student, a more fulfilled, complete person. Often we sat together and talked for hours about things like that—my relationship to school, to mankind, to the universe. It was eerie and deep and sometimes it made me feel a little confused, but then I felt in my heart that my happiness was all Faye ever considered. Man, it was a wonderful feeling in that period of my life to think that someone cared that much, that deeply about me, that I was important to someone! Special!

Sometimes it struck me as a little funny that Faye seemed a bit jealous of the boys I danced with at the school dances and even of my girlfriends, but that in a way made sense when I remembered how jealous I'd been of all Mom's friends. I had wanted Mom all to myself after the divorce, and I convinced myself that that was probably how Faye felt, that she needed someone to lean on, someone to depend upon, and man, that made me happy, thinking weak little me could give her strength.

Faye and I started going to plays and concerts and things together at the University. Some of them, in fact most of them, were big, hairy bores, but I thought Faye was trying to make me cultured and I wanted to be anything she wanted me to be. Sometimes people thought I was her daughter and that made me really proud. I fantasized about what it would be like being her daughter, being with her all the time. Mom was so busy with her job and her new boyfriend Nick and her silly girlfriend that she didn't have much time for me anyhow, especially since she had been promoted to second spot in her firm. Mom, big deal, big successful female executive who was so busy working she didn't have time for living, especially for her kid's living. I remember thinking Faye did more for me in a week than Mom did for me in a month.

One weekend Mom had to go to New York on company business and she asked me if I could spend the weekend with a friend. I talked to Faye

about it, and she invited me to come and stay with
her, cautioning me to let Mom think I was staying
at Laurie's or Dawn's house because, since they
didn't know each other, Mom might think it was
an imposition.

The week before Mom left was one of the long-
est weeks in my life for me, and Faye said it was
for her, too. We planned like two little kids looking forward to Christmas, passing each other
notes and sly glances. Imagine, a whole weekend
to talk. Maybe Faye could really explain to me
about transcendental "mediation," or whatever it
was that she loved, and I couldn't really understand at all. I remember I just kept writing on
every piece of paper that came under my pencil
"Wow! Oh Wow! Wow! Wow!" It was kind of
dumb and childish, but I truly thought something
wonderful and special was about to happen in my
life.

Friday afternoon, I told Miss Larsen, the gym
teacher, that it was my period and I really felt
rotten. Since it was my last class, she excused me
and instead of going to the nurse's office, I slipped
out and went to Faye's. She had bought some
flowers and had See's candy, my very favorite in
the whole world, and the refrigerator was stuffed
with all the junk food I had ever told her I liked.
To me it was like Christmas again in February. I
couldn't wait for her to get home. Home, that's

what I thought it was. After the divorce and Dad's leaving and Mom's new apartment and everything, I'd never had a home, a real home. But I did now . . . I did . . . I did, I told myself.

When Faye came in, we hugged and danced around the room till we fell in a tangled heap on the floor. She kissed my hair and eyes and nose the way my parents had when I was a little girl, and I felt I belonged.

Through that long weekend that passed like a minute, she snuggled me and protected me and told me how much she loved me and how important I was to her. Never once did she get sexy, but I could feel some new kind of force building inside of me that I had never felt. Oh, I'd gotten a little turned on before when we kids had looked at porno mags, or had speculated about what really went on in X- or double-X- or even triple-X-rated movies, and I'd had guys kiss me, even try to tongue me and get handsy. But somehow that had all seemed a little bit repulsive. I'd wondered then if there was something wrong with me and I wanted to talk to Faye about it over our weekend, but just the friendly togetherness of it was enough, and I didn't want to break the spell.

The following Saturday, Faye and I skied only two runs; then she asked me if I wanted to go "home." The look in her eyes kind of scared me, but I knew I wanted to go anyways.

After she'd made a big roaring fire, we sat on the floor and she kissed me on the lips for the first time. At first I trembled. It was different. I didn't want our relationship to change. I wanted to be her friend . . . her . . . I don't know . . . But she kept telling me to relax and how much she loved me and all that shit, and I believed her and trusted her. After just a little while she stopped and told me, just like my Mom, that all men were hard stools, just trying to hurt you and take advantage, that even little boys hit and punched people out when they got mad and that only women were gentle and caring.

By then it had gotten really hot in the room, so we took off our ski clothes and sat around in our underwear. She told me over and over what a beautiful body I had, and me with my skinny bird legs and flat front and no butt, I actually believed her after awhile. I felt like a thirteen-year-old Raquel Welch.

Faye got out her electric vibrator. Now that I'm an "into it" person, I can't believe the time and patience she took to turn me on. Actually she softened me up for over three months before she finally laid it to me. Man, when I want someone, I want them now! I don't want to fool around. I guess you know most gays are real single shots, picking up numbers in gas station rest rooms and stuff, but her, I dunno . . . I guess it was the big

171

conquest bit or something, but she really played it cool.

Well, we got it on regularly for the rest of the year. Her teaching me new tricks like a pet monkey, and me thinking it was all love and goodness and light and stuff. Shit, what a brainwash.

Mom was thrilled because my grades were good and I wasn't doping and climbing in bed with the boys. Dad, when I saw him, was so busy showing and telling me all the things he was and wanted to be that I think I could have told him right out and he wouldn't have heard me. He took me to football games and all the crap I hate, and just wanted to show me off like a toy he kept stacked away in a museum or someplace and brought out once in a while when the spirit moved him.

Once he introduced me to some fancy famous broad he was dating, and just to shock her, I gave her a little soul kiss. She pulled back and then gave me a tight little hug. "I do think I'm going to like your little girl a whole lot," she told Daddy. I cringed. She was the type of switch-hitting "ac/dc" Faye had told me about. I guess I had sensed it because ordinarily I'm so shy I'm afraid of my own shadow. Imagine *me* giving a stranger a soul kiss! But as time went on, I found that strangers are the only ones Lizzies feel really comfortable with.

But back to Faye. Just before school was out, she asked me if I wouldn't like to bring Laurie over. Laurie was almost a year younger than me, still twelve. It made me kind of cringe when I thought about it. I was enjoying sex like the greatest toy ever invented, but somehow I didn't want Laurie in the scene. Faye teased me and said I was just jealous, but that she'd show me how to break her in and we'd all three. . . . But crap, the more she talked the more she turned me off. Maybe I was just jealous that she'd like Laurie more than me. I didn't want that. More than anything else in the world I didn't want that because Mom and me were more and more at each other's throats every day. We were like two cats yowling and scratching. I couldn't do anything to please her, and she couldn't do anything to please me. Sometimes I actually hated her. Other times I wanted to run bawling to her telling her about the whole mess I was in and begging her to bail me out. Once I even tried to but the phone rang.

When school was out, I went to stay with Dad for two weeks. In a way I was glad because I was beginning to hate Faye, too, along with hating Mom and myself and everyone else in the world. It was a shit hole, and I was being bogged down and buried in it like quicksand. Maybe staying with Dad for good would be the way out.

One day I tried to talk to him about it. I asked

him if I could go to a psychiatrist because I was really crazy inside, and I couldn't live with myself, and I told him some of the things I'd done. He just tried to gloss over it and say his "precious angel" couldn't do anything bad enough to need a psychiatrist's help. Then he told me that all kids have their little periods of "sticky fingers" and their little experimentations with sex. He just wouldn't let me talk. He wouldn't! The harder I tried, the more he interrupted, telling me about his own sissy experiences and those of his friends and people he'd read about. I wondered if he was afraid to hear about me, what I'd done, what I was afraid I would do. Was the thought of that more than he could handle? Couldn't Mom handle it either? Was that why she turned me off? Was crazy mixed-up Faye the only one in the whole world I could talk to? Did I have to take her screw-up advice because there was no one else in the whole world who would even talk to me? When I got home, would she have little Laurie in her bed? Oh, crap, I couldn't stand that.

That night I tried to commit suicide with Dad's sleeping pills, but either he didn't have enough of them, or they weren't strong enough or something. It didn't work.

I begged him not to send me home to Mom and to the problem I didn't think I could live with, but he just lectured me about self-discipline and bought me a bunch of books about how to like myself and have confidence and all that shit.

Dad did let me stay two weeks longer than I was supposed to, and I really was feeling pretty good when I got home because he'd semi-promised me I could come back and live with him and go to school in the fall. But when I got home, Mom said that "Mrs. Stephens" had called a number of times and had even been over one day and had a long chat with her. Then she went on and on about what a lovely lady she was, and how lucky I was to have someone so cultured for a friend, someone who wanted to help me and "broaden my horizons."

I looked at my own Mother and couldn't believe it. My own Mother, trying to push me back into bed with the biggest, nastiest creature in the lagoon. I yelled that I never wanted to see that homo whore again, and Mom sent me to my room. She didn't even believe me!

The next two weeks of summer vacation were a bore. Thank God, Laurie had gone to her Grandmother's ranch for the summer. At least I didn't have to worry about that. Faye kept calling and sending me little girl presents. I guess my unavailability turned her on, like I was trying to turn myself off, but it was hard! Once you've been into the sex scene real good, it isn't all that easy to control your desires.

I tried to talk to Mom about homosexuals, but she just turned up her nose and said that was just too disgusting to even think about. She snickered that "nice girls" could tease about the "fruits" and the "tippie toed" boys, but beyond that she didn't think it was funny at all.

I remember as I lay in my room, hugging the teddy bear I'd had when I was little and crying into my pillow, that I had meant for our conversation to be anything but funny.

Wasn't there anyone who could understand me, would help me?

Just before school started in the fall, I met Mrs. Stephens in the Mall. Out of desperate loneliness and a desire not to make a scene, I went into The Topper with her to have a coke. That couldn't hurt, and besides, I'd have to see her everyday in the halls. Some time I'd have to learn to handle meeting her—Denver wasn't that big.

She was so kind and nice that when I got home, I wondered if my whole experience with her had been a nightmare. Had I flipped out of reality? Maybe she wasn't the monster I had made her out to be, maybe she hadn't really wanted little twelve-year-old Laurie sexually, maybe I had just brought that up from my own jealousies and fears and insecurities.

Two days later I met Faye on the bicycle path, and we spent the morning talking about nature and wondrous things that made life all worth living again. She wanted me to stay and have lunch with her at The Meat Ball, but I had promised Heidi I'd play tennis.

I think somehow Faye found out, I hope not from my Mother, but that is probably where she got it, that I rode my bike most Monday, Wednesday, and Friday mornings, as I was trying to improve my figure. Anyways, she always seemed to be there when I was.

One day we sat on the bank of the stream, and she told me how sorry she was that she had gotten me into something that I obviously was not ready for, or did not like, or felt guilty about. She promised me she would never mention it again and hoped we could continue to be friends. She told me that she had always before had older women lovers and seemed deeply and sincerely concerned that she had seduced me. That made me feel better because I hadn't ever wanted to believe that Laurie . . . I felt blood rushing up to my face. But when I thought about it, I was jealous of Faye's older women friends. I didn't want her to have anyone else. I didn't want her to have anyone, I broke down and sobbed, anyone but me. She understood, she cared . . . she was the only one at that point, who understood and cared.

On my fourteenth birthday Faye and I resumed our relationship. She could still send me flying through space, but now she made me do degenerate and debasing things to earn those highs.

I began to feel like a pit. There had to be another way. I certainly wasn't going to get Laurie for her, for us . . .

Tom lived on the corner from me. I knew he was into dope and asked him to get some for me. He offered to do even better, to take me to a kegger where I could have anything I wanted, and I wanted everything! I began using day and night. Cool . . . cool . . . cool.

Funny how Mom never suspected the Lizzie gig, but how soon she spotted my doping. The more she stayed on the rag, the heavier I used. I would sit in front of her so stoned that her lecturing didn't have any more effect on me than the drill at the dentist's when I was using gas. It was kind of nice and restful. I remember one time thinking I even kind of liked it when she hit me. Was that how it was when, sexually aroused, someone beat you? My mind was getting all jumbled.

Mom started hanging on the phone, tattling to Daddy about all the nasty things their little girl was doing, and Daddy even took time off from his precious work and came to get his baby and take her to another environment that would be more healthy.

Once there, and with me firmly imprisoned in

a fancy private girls' school, he went back to his own needs: money, money, money—power, power, power—women, women, women, and crumbs of time left over for me if there were any crumbs.

Within days the Lizzie set had found me. I'd been trying to hide my past and had turned over a new leaf and done all the things Daddy and Mommy had so tearfully advised me to do, cleaned up my act completely, language-wise, thought-wise, reading-wise, etc.—but the girls knew one when they saw one.

Six of us had been smoking a little pot down by the gardener's gate when Cheryl reached over and grabbed both my buns in her fists. "Man, I'd like to put those in my oven," she drooled. At first I tried to look shocked, then I recognized the clouded, lustful looks that hazed over each of their faces. Man, I'd gotten myself into a whole nest of them.

Fancy, expensive private school! Wow! If Daddy could only see the kind of education he was paying for and hear the standard joke, "Well, they're getting their money's worth. They're not going to have to worry about us getting pregnant and ruining their reputations."

By the time I was fourteen, I was well established in the gay community. Dad would drop me off at some of their dances and parties, and neat old square that he is, he wouldn't even be suspicious.

Sometimes when I was with him, I'd go in the ladies' room at the gas station and pick out the coded telephone numbers so I could call someone to come and pick me up in the lobby after I'd sneaked out of my room. Or I could get the numbers in any public telephone book scribbling. It was an exciting, adventurous way to live. And Dad and Mom were both proud as parents could be that I wasn't doping or boy beddin'.

When fall came, Dad decided I was strong and self-disciplined enough for public school; so I started my last year at junior high.

Things had been pretty dry while I had been vacationing for two weeks with Dad, then two weeks with Mom. I was ready for a little action. I hadn't planned on it being a real Italian macho-type neighborhood school, nor had I planned on being beaten up on, but I was. When I first started hanging out, both the straight girls and the straight guys took after us. We were really discriminated against, and even the teachers thought it was sport. There sure weren't any homos on the staff there. It was like all gays had signs on our backs. We got locked into toilets, pushed down stairs, chased by cars on the parking lot and every other kind of mistreatment. Within weeks the three gay guys in the school cut out, and another girl and me were begging our parents to transfer us.

Dad wouldn't, so I just didn't go. It was boring as hell just hanging around the apartment all day, answering the phone in a phony voice to tell the school why I was absent and intercepting the school mail.

At last in desperation I was back decoding the public phone books and rest-room walls. I was feeling worse about that all the time. I didn't want to come down with some damn social disease you couldn't ever get the hell rid of, and I was also beginning to feel that being gay, and maybe not completely in the closet any more, but anyway not proud of it, wasn't all that I wanted out of life.

One Sunday morning I saw a minister on TV and decided maybe, like he said, homosexuality wasn't what it was about after all. Sure, they wouldn't overpopulate the world, but then not a single one of the damn queers would ever have a baby of their own either. I began to think about how neat it had been when I was a little kid with a Mommy and a Daddy. What fun we had had. How loved and secure and forever we had been. If we had worked harder, could we all have made it last?

Before Dad got home I had cried myself to sleep and was still sobbing when he arrived. He picked me up like a baby and rocked me in his arms till I stopped trembling. I begged him to let me go to a psychiatrist, and finally he relented. His feeling was that only "real sickos" go to psychiatrists and that I was only a crazy, mixed-up kid. Little did he know.

I waited for my appointment like a prisoner must wait for a reprieve. I knew the doctor could straighten out my life. He had to. Should I really tell him every little detail like they did in movies and on TV? Would he be shocked and order me out of his office? Or run to the phone to call Mom and Dad? Well, if he did, he did. I had to talk to someone.

Dr. Jergenson seemed like a nice, gentle, caring man. The first three sessions he listened to my tearful story patiently and kindly, telling me "Yes," "Yes," "Yes," we could take care of all my problems and put my life on a safer, saner, happier keel.

I began to relax and really like him. Another month passed. I had gotten rid of all my mental garbage, and I felt better than I had in two years. Then he dumped all my garbage, plus more, back on my head at once. He wanted me to have sex with him to compare it with what I had had with women!

I ran out of his office gagging and screaming. Not only women were bastards, but men too. They all were! All humanity was!

I remember screaming and running down the street. I wanted people to hear me, to think I was crazy, wanted them to lock me up in some nice safe mental hospital where I would be protected and where someone would take care of me, feed me and clothe me and take care of me, not let me be hurt.

Hours later, completely exhausted, I let a policeman lead me back to Dad's apartment. I was fourteen years old and life really was not worth living. Dad hid his sleeping pills and his razor; so I tried to hang myself with my panty hose. Obviously that didn't work; I hadn't planned on them stretching so much.

All the psychiatrist told Dad was that I was a very sick girl. I didn't tell him anything. Why rake up the shit again? Why hurt him about something he couldn't or wouldn't do anything about anyways?

Dad sent me back to Nebraska to finish out the year with Grandma and Grandpa Ivy, and I'm really doing well. I think they're what it's all about. They haven't got much that's fancy, but we do corny things and play games and have fun; at least we do once a week on Monday nights. We call Monday night "home night" and it has to be next to a disaster to make us want to do anything else.

There's a girl my age next door, and she's so straight and naive she doesn't even know how cats have kittens. Oh, I shouldn't say that; I love her and she loves me. And sometimes I even go out with her brother Ked. The worst thing he's ever done is sneak a can of beer now and then. I try to act surprised and shocked, and I'm even beginning to sort of believe my own goody-two-shoes self-image. I hope Mom and Dad and Grandma and Grandpa will let me stay here till at least next year when I'm out of junior high. I think then maybe I can make it on the outs.

There are a few kids here who are not straight, and it's funny how you can spot them right off. It's a nonverbal kind of communication . . . maybe even advertising. I often wonder if other people can spot them as easily as I can. Faye told me one time she spotted me wanting her as much as she wanted me. Imagine! When I had just turned thirteen! I don't believe that now; I think she seduced me carefully and skillfully as she, and others like her, are probably even now seducing other kids.

O God, what's going to happen to me? Whatever, ever, ever, is going to happen to me?

I talked to this one counselor at that private school, and she said in some states like California it's O.K. to be a gay teacher, and that in other states they just cancel their teaching contract or don't renew it, and the queers just go on to other unsuspecting schools. Man, am I ever glad I don't have some little teen or preteen brother who's going to be seduced by some old dirty fag man. It's too embarrassing to talk about; so I guess he'd never tell anybody either, even if they would listen, which I doubt they would.

Oh, shit, life really is a mixed-up mess.

JANE
the price of peer pressure

My parents sent me to this youth conference to try
and straighten me out. Deep down in my heart I
know they'd do anything in the world for me, but
well, sometimes *they* just don't seem to matter, or
something inside me just wants to hurt them because I'm hurting so bad! I try not to think about
it; in fact, I've gotten to the point where I try not
to think about anything, just kind of float. It's
easier that way.

But let me answer your questions:

How were things when I was a little kid? I guess
I lived in a kind of ideal home, with kind of ideal
parents and ideal family. My Grandma Laura used
to take me to Santa Monica on the bus sometimes
just to go shopping. I thought it was lots of fun
transferring and walking from one store to another all over town looking for one special color
thread, or whatever she wanted. Grandma Laura

really loved me, and I guess I've never felt so bad and lost and lonely as I did when she died.

My Mom is really a neat musician and cook and just about everything. My two sisters and two brothers were all good students and popular and stuff. Naturally, we fought like all brothers and sisters do, but when the chips were down, we all stood together. None of them ever got into any big trouble. I don't know what happened to me. Could you tell I was the black sheep, or the bad seed, or whatever?

I know you're interviewing lots of kids here. But, well, some of them lead such peaceful nothing lives. I wish I could be like them, but there's this something inside me that craves excitement, and I guess I'm hyperactive or something. Barely existing just doesn't seem to be enough for me.

Oh, I loved my home. We had cats that always had kittens, and Blackie, a poodle that loved to take baths with me and had to be locked out of the bathroom, or he'd jump into anybody's tub. Some Sunday mornings we went out for hot doughnuts before we went to Sunday School, and Dad always teased me and spoiled me. Then, I thought I was his favorite. Later, I found all the kids felt the same.

Lots of Saturday mornings early, before practically anyone else got there, we'd go to the beach and have breakfast with my cousin's family—

bacon and eggs, ham and sausage, cinnamon rolls. Everything cooked on grills. Then we'd all play touch football in the sand, or dig sand crabs, or surf fish, or choose sides and see which team could make the biggest and fanciest castle or something.

After Sunday School, when we didn't go for doughnuts, my big family and the cousins I just told you about would all go to the Pickadilly for brunch. They were glad to see us, but they put us in the very back room because we were so loud and happy.

Were we rich? Not really, but then we weren't poor, either, I guess. Mom drove a Cadillac, and we had a maid one day a week. I don't remember ever having to do without anything I needed, but there were lots of things I wanted I didn't get.

You haven't asked me about the things I don't want to tell you. Would you promise on your sacred honor, on the Bible and on your own kids and on everything else in life that is important to you that you'd never let anyone in the whole world know that what I told you was about me, my real name, if I told you?

Oh, crap. I'm trying so hard not to think about it and pretending so hard that it didn't happen, but . . . well, I guess I was just a weak, rebellious smart ass who, like every other kid in the world that gets into trouble, thought it couldn't happen to me.

I grew up as a good member of the Church of ———, and there and at home I was taught from the time I was the littlest girl about stuff you should and shouldn't do. But things aren't all that easy and simple when you get older and have to make decisions for yourself about friends and really important things that will affect the rest of your whole life.

Sometimes I suspect it all started with my attitude when I was really young. Once when I was about, maybe nine or so we went to a talent show, and I remember this girl, about my age, singing like an opera star, and I just burst out laughing. My Mother was embarrassed and gave me a punch with her elbow, and my Dad told me when it was over that he considered my behavior "inexcusably rude." But I still went on telling everybody I knew how dumb the girl sounded and acted. I was kind of like that—always looking for things I could make fun of, being inconsiderate and unappreciative.

I never did like school. I would much rather have stayed home and played dolls and done all the fun things there were to do there. I remember when I was little asking my Mom *every morning* if I *had* to go to school. My first two, maybe three, teachers were the pits. They didn't like me, and I didn't like them; in fact they didn't like any of the kids. They just screamed and bawled us out and didn't make it any good time at all. The only things I liked were recess and when we had special programs and stuff. Being sent to school each morning was like being sentenced to another full day's punishment.

In about my third or fourth grade, I had one teacher who acted like she liked kids. She read to us and made learning kind of fun, but then the next year I got another always-on-the-rag type.

Did I ever talk much to my parents about school? No. What was there to say? They hated for me to be negative, and there certainly wasn't much of great happiness and cheer about going to the salt mines from 9:00 A.M. to 3:30 every day that I could tell them about. Each year it was more and more like being released from Siberia when the last bell rang.

In junior high I had one good teacher in art; then I found out that he was a queer, and that was the reason he was so sweetie pie. That kind of turned me off because he was being too good to my friend Donny, who lived just down the street, always taking him to football games and stuff. Sometimes it scared me and I wondered if all the stories I heard were true.

Well, in junior high, I, along with most of the other kids, started experimenting with dope. Some of them had started earlier, but then, I was kind of with the semi-conservatives. At the school dances it seemed like practically everybody there was stoned. Once I floated by our principal and wondered if all the adults hanging around, playing at being chaperones, didn't know, or didn't care.

I hated the slow dances because the guys were just trying to stroke their hard off. At least in my first and second year of junior high I hated it; by my third year I was beginning to like it.

To kind of build up to the dances, everybody who could dig them up brought *Hustler* and *Penthouse* and *Playboy* magazines in their notebooks. Sitting on the grass in front of school during lunchtime was a real ogling orgy. It was about this time that my parents really began to start wondering about me, worrying about my friends and my dirty mouth. I can't remember either one of them saying anything worse than "hell" or "damn" even when they smashed their fingers in the car door, or I bugged them to the point of no return.

My first year of senior high, I really started going with a bunch of sleazes. In one way my folks were kind of happy for me, because Joanie and Tina both belonged to the Pep Team, and their parents, although not members of our church or as active in the community as mine, were still successful and respected. Little did good old Mom and Dad suspect Joanie's and Tina's outside activities! Both belonged to the Junior Debs, which kind of made Mom hope maybe I would finally become interested in social things, but I never did. I couldn't relate to snotty girls trying to outdo other snotty girls.

In senior high our dances weren't as pornographic as the junior high ones with little kids practically "getting it on" right there on the floor with half the world, including some of their parents, watching them; but maybe that was because by now most of us had begun to have our love lives in less conspicuous places.

I don't remember exactly when I got sucked into sex, but once it happened, I was like an animal. It was the greatest invention since the wheel . . . since fire. I couldn't get enough of it.

I had been that way about drugs when I'd first started. "Christmas Glass" had become the thing I lived for. I'm sure I was high all the time for at least a month or more, and nobody did anything about it. My nice, square parents knew I was uptight and ragged at the least little thing, but that made them try even harder to be gentle and kind with me. Sometimes that made it worse, and I'd take more just to try and get some reaction out of them. I don't know what they could have done, but I wanted them to do something. Once my Dad, at his wits' end and having tried everything else, beat me, but even that didn't do any good.

I was going to do my thing no matter what!

My parents, especially my Mother, were really alarmed. They tried to get me to go to a private school. Mom even offered to move to another state with me, just the two of us, for one semester. She'd talked it over with Dad, and they were anxious to do anything to help me. But what?

Often I'd pass their room at night and see Mom kneeling by the side of her bed praying, with tears running down her cheeks, trying to wash away the dark circles under her eyes, or she'd scratch my back and beg me to try and help her figure out some way to make me "happy." She said "happy," but she really meant "good." I think she suspected a lot more than Dad did, but she tried to protect him as always.

There really wasn't anything anybody could pin on me. I was always in by ten-thirty on week-nights, and checked into the library and meetings just long enough to be seen. And on weekends I was always in by midnight, but how long does it take to go to someone's apartment and get loaded and . . . ? I try not to remember.

I'd seen enough burnouts and OD's to be really, really leery of drugs, along with all the information we got in classes about chromosome damage and brain damage and stuff, most of us turned to booze, which has been around since the beginning of time. In fact we laughed about how old Noah got smashed out of his gourd right after he got the ark landed.

I had a cast-iron stomach, and while some of the other kids got sick, I never did. I just drank more and more of anything anybody had and got more and more turned-on by sex.

I'm trying hard to be straight now. I really am; then it was like . . . well, like the worst hunger in the world. I'd . . . O God, I'm so ashamed . . . I'd get it on with anybody, anytime, any place.

Now sometimes I wonder how come I didn't get pregnant, and I really worry that maybe I'm sterile and I'll never be able to have any babies. Honestly, I don't know whether it makes me feel better to talk to someone about all my past shit, or if it just turns both our stomachs and seems like more X-rated stuff that decent people are trying to get rid of. I don't want *anyone* to go through what I've been through if I can help them. I don't want *anyone* to suffer what I'm suffering now, if maybe reading about it is the answer. I wonder if it would have helped me if I could have read about it, if it would have made me go to my bishop or to a psychiatrist or . . . something . . . anything. Then, even then, during my worst times, I knew I needed help, I wanted help, but I was scared to death I might get help, too. Being hooked on sex is like being hooked on drugs; you really can't help it, or you don't want to. I was going to church regularly with my parents and with some of the kids who were leading the same two-sided life I was, playing Righteous Ruthie and Holy Harry and being sex fiends at the same time.

Once I went home with Marty, whose Mother worked. He was only twelve years old, and I raped him—actually raped him! Can you believe that of a girl from a nice family like mine? Another time at a party I not only took on a kid my age but also his Dad. How's that for being a cheap whore. And once, even worse than that, Joanie and I had guys lined up between two vans at the drive-in, trying to see who could service the most in an hour.

Did I ever feel guilty? Sometimes I'd feel so bad, so humiliated and embarrassed I couldn't bear it and I'd literally beat at myself. Then I'd go right ahead like I did the Saturday night in the van and the next morning rip off to Sunday School. Do you think doping really made me crazy? It must have; else how could I, from my background, have acted like that! But guilty, I don't think during that whole time I felt real guilt; it was like, well, I'd convinced myself that everybody was doing it, everybody I knew was. No, that's not true, most of the kids who went to church weren't. I was, well, I was just trying to convince both my parents and myself that I could go with both the soshes and the sleazes at the same time and still be my own person. What a lie. What a laugh.

Once my parents were gone, and Terry, the hippie brother of one of our neighbors, and I made it on every bed in our house. Afterwards I remember I felt that I had desecrated a holy place, and I knelt down and wept and prayed, but my prayers didn't get through any more; it was like I was praying to the mattress.

The Hurleys, a very wealthy couple in our area, lived in New York, but kept an apartment for themselves and their friends when they came to Southern California. Neil's Dad ran the property management company that handled their apartment, and as they were rarely there, we high school kids used it as our party pad. Even a roach burn could be blamed on someone else's use and written off on an insurance claim.

I hate that apartment now. It's where a lot of us got started, kind of lured away from everything some of us had ever been taught and into all kinds of degenerate things. But with the kind of show-how magazines they have now, even the most frigid of old maids, especially if she'd had enough vodka mixed with coke, would get turned on.

Tell you about the magazines? Well, for instance, *Hustler** and *Chic,* they're most kids' favorites, have close-ups of all kinds of male and female parts. Once there were cartoons of the President's wife's breast cancer, and all kinds of sickie nudes like one woman almost nine-months pregnant, and a girl being raped by a snake. You wouldn't believe things like janitors sweeping shit out of rest rooms—just plain shit, and "getting it on" with animals, and castration and stuff.

Where do kids get such magazines? No problem. If you can't buy them yourself, there is always an older kid or adult who will get them for you.

Do I think my friends had anything to do with my problems? Oh, yeah. I wouldn't listen to my parents when they tried to tell me that you can't be surrounded on all sides by chicken shit and not get some on you; that's not exactly what they said, but whatever it was they said, it meant the same thing. Nobody could tell me anything then. It was like talking to a deaf person. You can't hear if you won't listen.

Actually, it's strange but true that good kids are

Hustler has a circulation of nearly 2 million. *Playboy* is first with 5.7 million; *Penthouse* is second with 4.6 million. Larry Flynt, who owns *Hustler,* claims that it and *Chic,* along with the kinky sexual devices they advertise, netted him $20 million last year.

always trying to reenforce each other's strengths, and rotten kids are always trying to tear down each other's reserves. Like shoplifting and booze and doping and sex and stealing cars and everything else you can think of, are all sort of in the same package. Most kids that will do one will eventually do any or all. And it's like when you're with the rowdies, they kind of turn off all your alarm systems, or maybe you do it yourself. Anyway, I remember when I was little, oh, maybe six or so, I stole two candy bars. Mom marched me right back to the store and made me go through one employee to another explaining exactly what I had done until I got to the very head of the big store himself. In his office I felt about an inch high, and I really did mean I'd never steal again when I cried for forgiveness and promised I wouldn't. That little episode all became a big joke later when I really got into stealing anything I wanted, especially when I was with any of my "marvelous" peers. There wasn't anything we wouldn't do, and some of them were the supposed "cream" of the school. I wasn't. I'd never had much confidence, and I'd never felt I could belong to all the soshie things; so I just pretended I didn't want to. I was loud and aggressive, but that, too, was just kind of a cover-up, I-don't-care attitude to get attention.

We did terrible kinds of vandalism things, too,

like burning benches in the park and on purpose stuffing up the school toilets and stuff.

Once it was ironic when a bunch of people from the church were asked to help clean the city parks, and our family went to clean up a mess of things that me and my crappy friends had made the week before, things I wouldn't have done in a million years if I hadn't been with those friends. When you're with a bunch of kids that say something is all right, it seems all right, especially if you're stoned or you've been drinking. It's so crazy! You convince yourself, honestly, that everybody's doing it, and it's true that everybody you know is doing it; but that's because you're going only with sleazes, crap-outs that don't care about you or them or anything else except a little "now" excitement and stimulation.

That park thing was really a bummer. Gross things sprayed all over, toilets and sinks stopped, benches bent and broken, swing ropes cut, nails hammered through a slippery slide, with the sharp ends up. I couldn't believe I'd been a part of doing it; in fact I got sick just looking at it, and Mom had to take me home.

Everybody had told me I couldn't play in the sewer without getting shit on me, but smart ass me, I knew better than they did. Yeah, I did! Will sleazes pick you up when you stumble? Shit, no! They just push you down deeper in the hockey and rub your face and nose in it. What I'm really trying to say, I guess, is that you really can't go with sleazes and soshes. You can't be good and bad at the same time. It's kind of like trying to go in two directions at once . . . up and down. Believe me, there is no way! I've tried! And now I'm so damned far down I'm not sure I'm ever going to be able to make it back up even to where normal people exist. I'm so weak I know there's no possible chance without a lot of good help from a lot of good friends. And who'd want me for a friend with my background, my reputation. But anyway, I know there's no way I can make it alone.

Dear God, how I wish I knew what was going to happen in my future! But then again, maybe I don't want to know. Maybe I couldn't stand to know. I guess I've got to keep hoping and praying that this youth conference can reshuffle my brains like my parents are hoping it will.

TWO YEARS LATER

MARY—*about cults*

Talking about my old cult days is almost like talking about an old movie. It's real, but it isn't real, and sometimes I'm not sure I remember every little sequence. Well, anyway, it's like any experience you have in life; you either grow from it, or it holds you back. But it hasn't held me back. In fact, I've become a crusader for deprogramming. I'm going to college part time and working even harder on this side of the fence than I did on the other. No, that's impossible; in cults you give twenty-four hours, seven days a week, and that's not good for your mental or your physical health. Anyway, I'm taking night classes, and eventually I'll be a social worker working full time with deprogramming.

You want to know what kinds of kids get into

cults? Well, it's really funny about the caliber of
kids who are open to them. They're not the disad-
vantaged or the ghetto, for they're on to "hus-
tlers" and are too "street-smart" to be taken advantage of and used. Most kids drawn to the
movements are serious kids, seriously searching
for something to believe in, something with a real
purpose to be dedicated to. Basically, they are
upper-middle-class whites, from maybe sixteen—
seventeen—eighteen—to twenty-three or so.
They are very loving and giving people who have
a strong need of peer approval. Without excep-
tion, they want to see a better world and often
prefer simplistic answers to complicated questions, even if they're far out. They're kids looking
for someone who will take away doubts and give
them assurance and something worthwhile to believe in.

They aren't the seconds, or the rejects, or the
failure people, as most everybody seems to think.
They're mostly nice, average kids from nice, average homes, kids who are just going through a
period of trying to find themselves, who they are,
what they're doing here, where they're going.
Most of them are idealistic, so idealistic in fact that
they are looking for things that are unrealistic.
Like me, for instance. My parents were good,
concerned, nice people; but I was going through
a self-critical, parent-critical age where they

couldn't have pleased me no matter what they had done. I didn't want to be pleased. In deprogramming I've learned that I was not only *not listening,* I was seeing my parents as I wanted to see them. I remember I thought of them as plastic people in a plastic environment. Actually, our apartment was a luxury apartment with heavy carpeting and plush furnishings and drapes. And my parents were very concerned human beings, caring, and more than caring, *doing something* about social pressures and scholastic things and general good causes. I don't know why I put them down so at that age unless I was just going through my general put-down period about everything, including myself. Now I wonder what I expected them to be like—dancing in the hall and over the furniture like the old Fred Astaire-Ginger Rogers movies maybe.

There are usually symptoms in kids who are making an opening in their lives for cults, kids who have become somewhat "loners," who are "in between" semesters, boyfriend, or girlfriend relationships, jobs, etc. Kids who are changing normally established patterns in their lives are the most vulnerable. Little by little, breakdowns erupt in home communications, then in-growing attitudes—that society is evil, and that it's virtuous to destroy society because of those evils. It's about here that a kid is really open to other kids on the street who are recruiting.

Adults would be amazed at how open kids can be about talking to strangers. Members of cults, particularly the Moonies and Hare Krishnas, as well as most others, have been thoroughly schooled in how to reach young people. They know their needs—like their longing to be associated with a group of other young people doing something *constructive* in a world that seems mainly destructive. There's a technique of these groups—winning friends and influencing people, making you feel important, that you can belong to something good. Nothing new, just finely honed salesmanship. They're trained to treat you as if you're the most important person in the world. They reinforce your goals and offer you a way of attaining them with no obvious pressure. In fact, they are so skilled at manipulation that they make you *want* to join them. They've been carefully schooled, too, not to mention that they're from the Church of God, or the Unification Church, or the International Society for Krishna Consciousness, or the Forever Family, the Divine Light Mission, the Federation for Victory over Communism, God's Light Infantry, Scientology, Love Israel, The Assembly, The Body, The Farm, The Way, One World Crusade, Life's Family, or any of the other cults flourishing actively all over the world.

Some cults are more destructive than others. For instance, Carol Kay was sent to us to be reprogrammed from the Love Israel Family in Seattle. At first she told us she had died in her past and was living with the Love Israel Family in Heaven. Bringing her back to earth was absolute torment for her. She wanted her "God-centered family" and wept and pleaded for them. Her own family she had completely rejected. At this point Carol Kay truly believed that their leader was Christ, their Savior, their King, and their Father come again upon this planet.

She had also been programmed to believe that death is an illusion, that she would never age, that she was timeless. She believed and acted like a little child. All ego and personality had been lost in total oneness of the group. She kept saying, when we were trying to get her to think again for herself, make her own decisions independent of us, independent of them, that "I can't let my own little mind get in the way. I must always use my big mind, the Family mind. My little mind is unimportant. It will lie to me. My big mind, the Family mind, is the only one I can depend on."

If we pushed, she had been taught to "blank herself out," so there were times when literally no one could get through to her. It was as if she were in a coma.

As Carol Kay began to look at things for herself

"with her own little mind," she said woman's role is to serve men and give birth to children; that was the Love Family teaching. Also that women do not raise their own children. Parental ties are eliminated, and the word "mother" is an abomination. Attachment to parents, established religions, education, and society as a whole all have to be destroyed for complete control.

If Carol Kay had had a child while in the cult, it would not be hers but would come from the temple and belong to the Family.

Two of the Love Family cult, she said, died from inhalation of toluene in a religious rite. Two cult leaders called Serious and Strength say: the fact that the world considers a substance deadly or harmful meant little to them; that society's laws have made criminals out of people who are only exercising their constitutional right to the pursuit of peace of mind and their own kind of happiness. They chose to experiment with tell-u-all, a legal substance, rather than those they considered more desirable and safer, but which were illegal, such as LSD, peyote, and others. Carol Kay is having a hard time coming back. She still will not touch money and will not talk to a man unless spoken to. She will eat only one-third as much as a man because "I am only one-third of a man." She seems to have no individualism or identity. She has given up the character of her being. Carol Kay is like one of the robots in the movie about the Stepford Wives.

How many cults are there? There are 250 fairly large cults operating in the United States; all together there may be up to 2,500, some with only a few members, others like Scientology having hundreds of thousands. Between two and three million people in this country belong to cults, mostly impressionable kids eighteen to twenty-four.

Cults are big business like, for instance, the Brotherhood of the Sun in Santa Barbara, California. They have an organic produce market and a warehouse and gross about three million dollars per year, all with absolutely free help.

Reverend Sun Myung Moon of the Unification Church has thousands of kids working as slave-laboring migrant workers. "Moonies" also have contracts to do custodial work in the Sacramento, California, State buildings as well as in many others. All monies received are turned over, one hundred percent, to Reverend Moon, "The Messiah, the Son of God." The Hare Krishna kids sell incense, books, magazines, ginseng tea, and flowers, and solicit offerings for lying causes—children's clinics, medical facilities in distressed lands, drug centers, among others.

The cult recruiter, whether it be on a campus or on a street corner, is usually seen by the mark as being exceptionally friendly, tranquil, and sincere. This raises the mark's sense of curiosity and intrigue. The recruiter seems almost the opposite of the chaos the marks are feeling. They want to find out what the recruiter knows that they don't; so when they are invited to the center to a "feast," they gladly follow, believing innocently that they are going for a philosophical discussion, to see a movie, etc.

Most adults find it hard to understand how kids get into cults, but it happens so innocently. Let me tell you what Pete Johnson, sixteen, who escaped from the Hare Krishna cult, says:

"On my school vacation last summer, I was invited to spend a weekend at a Krishna temple and learn something about their religion. I rose at 3:00 A.M. to chant prayers, and for several hours during the day I practiced 'gapa,' which is chanting prayers almost silently to oneself. This has a strong self-hypnotizing effect. Immediately I said I would stay a little longer. I was sent to another temple in Portland, Oregon. That's when the mind takeover really began.

"My head was shaved, except for one lock. I was given Hindu robes and beads to wear. The immediate effect was to isolate me from my former self. I was allowed no newspapers, and was completely cut off from the outside world. Then the brainwashing began in earnest.

"It was hammered into me that all my life outside the Hare Krishna cult was an illusion—my parents, the rest of the world. Only the cult was good, and the only way to serve God was to give myself totally up to the cause of the cult.

"Any food other than the cult's vegetarian diet was sinful. To sleep more than six hours a night was sinful.

"I must have passed the test, for I graduated to the real object of the cult—harvesting money. Three or four of us would make up a team, and on weekends we'd haunt the center of a town. We'd hand a passerby a flower and ask for a donation. My team's average weekend take was $600, which we handed over to the temple 'president.' We drew no pay ourselves.

"The Hare Krishna cult is run by an Indian magazine publisher, A. C. Bhaktivedanta Swami Prabhupada. Eighty years old, he arrived in the U.S. in 1965 with $5 in his pocket. He started chanting in New York's Central Park, and young people began following him. Now he has temples all over the United States and Europe, and he's a multimillionaire.

"He teaches the 'Absolute Truth' philosophy, which is that everything is an illusion except his views. Of course, it is no illusion that the Swami runs around in a Rolls Royce and flies all over the place collecting money.

"They programmed me so my own mind wouldn't let me out. Mind control is a scary thing; I have firsthand knowledge of it now. The brainwashing methods used by the cults should be made known, so that parents can see what is being done to their children."

Another case is Marie, a nineteen-year-old girl we just deprogrammed. She's fairly typical. She had this friend at school who one day started talking to her about Jesus. She was really interested because she was a Catholic, and there were lots of questions her church didn't answer. The girl asked Marie to go up to the San Bernardino mountains for a weekend retreat, but she was on the swimming team at Santa Monica City College, so she couldn't make it. The girl called every day for two weeks, just being friendly and continuing to extend the offer; then she called three times a week, and after six weeks she was still calling once a week.

Finally, a time came when Marie could get away. Some people picked her up in a van and took her to a big old house in Hollywood. There a girl talked to her about her past life and answered questions. They talked about everything, including old movies, then twenty-five of them went up to an old YMCA camp. All the way up they talked about motorcycles and such. A really nice girl, Erica came out to meet Marie at the camp and just took her over. She was caring and friendly. They talked about God and ideals, and while Marie had been a little scared at first, she was soon made to feel accepted and at ease.

In the afternoon there was a lecture, and each person was asked, "If you could have anything you wanted at this very moment, what would it be?" Marie said it would be to know God personally. Then they were taught the Beginning of the Divine Principle of the Creation and called to action. The call was, Marie said, exciting and motivating. "Being active for good" sounded exactly like what she wanted out of life.

There was so much love and support during the weekend that every time she had a negative reaction, she thought she must be bananas because everyone else was so happy and content. After the three days, Marie still wanted to know more; so she went home and got some clothes and came back for seven more days, even though she had registered for the new term and should have started school. At the retreat, each evening she was asked to write her feeling about the day and ask questions. She was also supposed to pray and ask God about these things to see if they were true. Everyone was so nice, so attractive, so involved, so dedicated, so happy, playing volleyball and having fun. It seemed like they had no problems, no pressures. After evaluation, her questions were each answered, so simply that when she didn't understand an answer she felt that she was just dumb, and didn't push.

After her first three days she noticed that only about 20 or 25 percent of the kids who came up stayed. After seven days about 80 percent of the remainder stayed, and after twenty-one days those left became members.

It was not until Marie's sixth day at camp that she found out that the sponsor of the retreat was the Unification Church of Reverend Sun Myung Moon, and that he was considered to be "The Messiah, the Son of God."

After that lecture they were told they were going to start studying their Holy Father's life (meaning that of Reverend Moon), and always they added that if one wasn't sure he was the Messiah, that person should leave the room. They also began ending all prayers by saying, "not in the name of Jesus Christ," but "in the name of our true Parent, Reverend Moon."

Marie had some little frightening reservations at first, but everyone else seemed so happy and tranquil, a part of her felt privileged to be in the room, so she stayed.

On the tenth day, Marie's Mother called the camp, but before Marie was given the phone she was given a legal-sized page filled with stock answers for any questions her Mom might ask: "I've found a new life, God needs me," etc.

Marie was taught that time was short, and after one learns the truths they *must* help solve the world's problems. God had had no help on earth for almost 2,000 years. Now He had "the Messiah," Reverend Moon. Marie says she was so brainwashed at this point she felt she couldn't take off even one day to explain to her Mother.

After two weeks Marie went home again, sold the car her Dad (her parents were divorced and her Dad lived in Ohio) had given her for a graduation from high school present. She also sold all her records and material things and returned with the money she had raised. She wanted to make a clean break, let God know she would do anything, give anything for Him!

She was taught that Reverend Moon and the people in her group were her real family, and that she didn't need "earthly family" any more. She had gone beyond that. Now her call was to raise money for the cause. Time passed, and Reverend Moon needed more people to raise funds in New York, and since Marie had been very effective, she was sent there to train others. Marie, who had never been out of the Los Angeles area, was amazed and awed by Tarrytown where Reverend Moon owns seven estates, but her indoctrination there was completely different. Mr. Aidenberry from England bellowed at them: "You stink as far as God is concerned! If you think, even in the slightest, about loving someone else, *anyone else* in the whole world other than Reverend Moon, you are making God cry!"

Thirty people had come from Los Angeles for the new drive, and Marie and her team went to Philadelphia. She pushed her group to go forty hours without sleep, fund raising. She was caught in an almost Pavlovian vise: acceptance and security if she pleased, threats of eternal rejection if she did not.

Once Reverend Moon caught a tuna and gave it to their house. She felt so privileged, she on her knees, prayed three straight hours before she could even touch it.

Before a big rally at Yankee Stadium for extra fund raising, each group started a forty-day fast. After fasting for forty hours each, someone else would take over. Every thought of Marie's was now turned in to "What would Father want? How would Father feel? What would Father do? How could she serve him? What did she have to give him?"

She was sent back to Huntington Drive in Pasadena. While there, she contacted her Mother about the pearls her Grandmother had left her. They were in her Mother's safety deposit box, and she wanted to turn them over to Reverend Moon.

Through the letter her Mother had her picked up and deprogrammed.

Her cult period Marie now calls her "zombie" years. She cannot understand how, for that time she sincerely believed as they told her that Mr. Moon had succeeded where Christ failed. Yes, that he had succeeded where Adam and Eve failed, where Abraham and Jacob failed, where Mary and Joseph failed, where everyone failed except the "Divine Father" Reverend Moon. She feels repelled too, that she prayed in Moon's name instead of Jesus Christ's and that she recruited "slave labor" and helped raise hundreds of thousands of dollars for Moon's own personal use through deceit.

She is beginning to understand that the cult strategy is to reduce the amount of sleep and the caloric intake of the initiates to make them more docile and controllable. The tremendous peer pressure to agree with the group and not to disagree with the group, and the constant chants to focus their attention and limit peripheral vision both physically and psychologically until their worlds become tunnel-visioned.

Like horses with blinders on, new devotees are kept on the cult's prescribed paths, and distractions from the sidelines are blocked out. The kids are continually reinforced in these beliefs by everything in the cult environment. And because the environment is so limited and controlled, they can be given completely new identities. Their past, their culture, everything but the now, becomes unreal, unimportant. Names are changed, so too, is manner of dress. With the Hare Krishnas, the hairstyles, ways to tell time, the underwear, the way they eat their food—even the farina they get in the mornings they eat with their fingers off a piece of paper laid on the floor —everything is changed to make one forget the past.

Kids are programmed to do absolutely only, and without question, what they're told to do, which is ironic because in their own homes most of them found even the slightest order most difficult. Anyway, at a Queens County, New York, grand jury hearing, one former Hare Krishna devotee testified under oath that she even, without question, drank cow's urine during a group ritual.

The most frightening aspect to me is that this cult-diseaselike phenomenon is spreading like a contagious thing. You're just as likely to have a kid come up to you on North Audley Street in England as on Madison Avenue in New York City, selling candles, or candy, or flowers, or ginseng tea, claiming untruthfully that the money is going to charity, or to send kids to camp, or to build buildings for drug addicts, or medical centers in underdeveloped countries.

And it's heartbreaking to work with embittered kids like Barrie Baer, twenty-two, who worked seven days a week for room and board only, after she joined Divine Light Mission—the cult's main object in her was harvesting money.

Many people discount the fact that brainwashing, programming, and self-hypnosis are possible, but they are! The Los Angeles police, as well as any number of others, are using hypnosis to help with some of their cases. In Hare Krishna many, many pages of their book, the *Bhagavad-Gita,* as it is called (the abridged edition with translations and elaborate purports by his Divine Grace A. C. Bhaktivedanta Swami Prabhupada) deals with putting oneself "in a constant state of trance"— another word for hypnosis—and staying in it. Each day for two hours, one hour in the morning and one hour at night, as well as at times in between, devotees of Hare Krishna are supposed to chant either to themselves or aloud, "hare krishna hare krishna krishna krishna hare hare hare rama hare rama rama rama hare hare," which means loosely that they are thinking only of Krishna, being absolutely and completely unselfish, selfless, doing only for him with no thought for themselves, or anything, or anyone else in the world outside them, or the world within them.

On page 25 of the *Bhagavad-Gita* the Hare Krishna devotees are told they must rise above sense perception like heat and cold, happiness and distress, that they must learn to tolerate without being disturbed. This is the reason the Krishnas can put twenty-one young women or men in a very small drafty room in seven three-tier bunks with only a sleeping bag for each.

On page 33 Krishna devotees are programmed to forsake their parents and background. It says if they are completely surrendered to Krishna consciousness, they are no longer obliged to anyone, kinsmen, humanity, nor forefathers, that their real parents and family are a "skin disease."

On page 36 they are told to block out their past existence, that when their intelligence has passed delusion, they will become indifferent to all that has been heard or will ever be heard.

On page 37 they are taught that the mind will no longer be disturbed when it remains fixed in the trance of self-realization, for then they will have attained the divine consciousness; and that when they give up all varieties of sense desires, when they are not elated when happy, free from attachment, fear, and anger, they are merged in transcendence.

On page 41 they are taught again how to give up all desires for sense gratification so they can have real peace.

On page 85 they are programmed to believe that when doubting Hare Krishna, there will be no happiness in this world nor in the next.

On pages 99, 100, 101 they are taught to stay in a constant trance, that they should not rejoice upon achieving something pleasant nor should they lament about something unpleasant. Such a person, they teach, is always in a trance, enjoying the pleasures within. They should sit, shutting out all external sense objects, and with their eyes closed should concentrate between their eyebrows controlling inward and outward breathing, thus becoming free and liberated.

On page 107 kids are taught to hold up their heads erect and stare at the tips of their noses, which will subdue the mind, make it devoid of fear, and make them completely free from sex life. Through controlling the body, mind, and activities, they can attain the kingdom of God.

On page 168 devotees are conditioned to nonattachment to children, wife, home, and so on.

On page 266 there is a summary of the teachings. One can attain perfection by:

1. Giving up all objects of sense gratification.
2. Being free from attachments, parents, family, things.
3. Eating only "a small quantity of food."
4. Being "always in a trance."

219

Oh yes, in Plate 43 it says that at death the living consciousness will carry what he is to his next body through reincarnation; if a person eats at all more than is needful, he will come back as a pig, if he is at all lustful, he will come back as a dog, etc.

How difficult is it to deprogram? I don't really like the word deprogramming. It sounds like more of what the cults are doing, reversed. Actually, we just try to get kids to start thinking for themselves again instead of being like docile, obediently trained animals. Often when kids first come to us, they have difficulty even making the decisions between white and wheat bread.

People, especially kids, have the right to know what "mind control" is all about, and how effectively and easily it works. Most think they are impervious to brainwashing; yet it's happening in the tiniest, subtlest ways all the time, like going to the market and buying some gook that you don't really want, but that has been heavily advertised on TV, or similar to meeting a high-pressure salesman on a car lot.

Most of the professional people I've heard lecture think it is possible, given total control of a person's environment, to turn his mind in a very short period of time, especially if that person's ego structure isn't too well developed.

You can't imagine how awful it is having tortured parents come in pleading for help, or seeing a Mother running up to a Hare Krishna on the streets, describing her daughter and pleading for any kind of lead as to her whereabouts, weeping and promising she won't cause any trouble. You look into the devotee's eyes and see only a desire to get away. The Mother might as well be speaking in a foreign language or be invisible. She, her daughter, everything that might hurt or distract, has been programmed out of the cult kid's life. I know! And I bleed because I know!

What happened to Sky, the head of the group I belonged to? I heard that he'd gone to Switzerland to live royally for the rest of his life off the money he'd put in Swiss accounts, off our labors, but I try not to think about it.

Sorry, I gotta go now; that call was about a little sixteen-year-old girl they just brought in who has been programmed to think that her parents, as well as the deprogrammers, are Satan's tools, and are going to torture and then kill her.

MARK—*about suicide*

Mark committed suicide.

The suicide rate among young people doubled in the 70's.

It has tripled since the 60's.

In 1977 it is the third major cause of death.

The suicide rate is *200 times greater than it was ten years ago!*

Fifty percent of all kids think about suicide at least once a month as a way to get out of stress.

Ten percent of the kids who try suicide eventually make it.

Reasons given by young people and professional people in the field for the growth in suicide, not just in the U.S. but throughout the world, include the following:

The change in the family home structure.

The breakdown in stable family life.

The great number of children who live in a one-parent home.

No security. No support.

No one noticing the signs: "I'm depressed." "I'm lonely." "I'm ill." "Help me." "I can't relax." "I don't have anyone to talk to." "No one listens." "No one understands." "I'm not important." "I can't relate." "NO ONE CARES!" "NO ONE CARES!" "NO ONE CARES!"

Teachers have such heavy class loads they can rarely work on a one-to-one basis.

Disturbed families produce disturbed children.

Social pressures have made friends afraid to be "all out vulnerably self-sacrificingly friendly."

Mark's Mother gave me the suicide note which Mark's Father had given to her:

DEAR ANYBODY:

IF ANYBODY CARES PLEASE STOP ME.
PLEASE, PLEASE STOP ME! PLEASE DAD
. . . PLEASE MOM . . . PLEASE KATIE . . .
PLEASE RELATIVES . . . PLEASE TEACHERS
. . . PLEASE RELIGIOUS PEOPLE . . . PLEASE
GOD. I'VE NEEDED YOU ALL. I STILL NEED
YOU. ANYBODY. PLEASE . . . PLEASE HELP
ME.

My youngest daughter, when reading Mark's
follow-up, made an interesting observation:
"Mom, *who* do you think really killed Mark?"

MILLIE—about homosexuality

So many things have happened in the past two
years. I remember when I talked to you then I felt
so trapped and unhappy, so miserable and lost and
despicable, desperately wanting answers, desperately wanting security, desperately wanting to be
loved, and not knowing where to go for any of
those things. In my first year of high school I
became even worse. I was really a sixteen-year-old
sleaze, getting names from public rest rooms and
scribbles on walls and in phone books and stuff—
just hopping from bed to bed with anyone who

would turn down the covers, or having quickies in public toilets or any other place, sometimes for money, sometimes for fun, sometimes just to have someone close to me even for a moment.

In junior high it had been kind of tough because I hadn't quite known how to handle things, but by tenth grade. . . . I can't even think about it without getting sick to my stomach.

I know I don't have to talk if I don't want to, but if what happened to me can help even one kid know what kind of a degenerate world that is, without having to go there, I'll crawl on my belly over broken glass, naked, to tell them about my experiences.

You wouldn't believe how the gay groups are growing in high schools and junior highs; it's like an epidemic, and I guess switch-hitting is even bigger. But it's no wonder with everybody telling kids, "If it feels good, do it" and "If you don't use it, you lose it" and all that kind of junk that we just can't handle. Then I was really grooving on that kind of garbage and . . .

I don't know what would have happened to me if I hadn't met Richard Done. Honestly, he's the very, very greatest! One day at school one of the kids mentioned him. He works as a counselor at The Happy House, which is kind of a hangout for kids with drug and related problems. Out of sheer desperation I decided to go there, even pretending to be hung up on drugs myself if that was necessary, but drugs had never been too much my thing, at least not something I couldn't handle.

Well, anyway, the first night a bunch of us just sat around and strung each other; then the second night I began to feel more secure. These kids really weren't shitting each other; they were sincere. Man, after the "mothers" I'd been going with, I couldn't believe it. A bunch of kids just like myself, just as lost, just as lonely, just as hurting. It didn't really make any difference *why;* it was just important that we, each in our own way, needed something, someone! Our past problems weren't the things any more. The question was how could we help each other out of the pits.

After a few more sessions Richard took me home one night to baby-sit for him. I couldn't believe it, the love and respect he had for Jeannie, his wife. Man, he treated her like every woman wants to be treated, oh, not like she was a sacred something, but with a sense of humor and respect and . . . I don't know . . . But from the very beginning I felt it was good, except that then I hadn't learned to trust, and I kept waiting for her to make a move on me, or him. I knew deep inside they wouldn't, still . . . I dunno . . . it's hard to explain changing one culture pattern for another, going from the land of the kinkies to the home of the straights.

Not that my parents weren't straight. Now that I look back, I can see they really tried in their own way. They never did abuse me or neglect me or . . . well, it was more like they didn't hurt me, but they didn't nurture me either. Is that the right word? "Nurture" seems like something you do with sick plants or sick people, but maybe I was sick, I guess actually I was, sick in the head and in the heart and guts too. Down where it really hurts!

No, my parents never did know about my Lizzy days; in fact they always thought I was mostly a good, easy-to-manage girl. I've heard them tell their friends lots of times that they wouldn't have been able to handle it if I'd been like other kids, you know, junkies and all-night runaway type whores and stuff. With me, on the surface I was always a conformist. If they could only have seen underneath.

Back to Richard and Jeannie. Sometimes the three of us would discuss me for hours. They cared! I knew they cared! They wanted me to be straight and happy like they were, with a couple of little kids and a real purpose in life, instead of just floating from one experience to another. They wanted me to see a man and wife working together with their family against the world, instead of just floating from one experience to another.

In my loneliness it wasn't what they said that impressed me so much as what they did, and how they acted, a permanent kind of accepting the worst and making the best of each other. And there was no being ashamed or insecure about their relationship. They were proud and eager to be together anywhere, any time. They were loving and helping, not hurting and using.

I think the hardest part of my rehabilitation was self-forgiveness, and I'm not sure I've really mastered that. I still feel guilty when I think about the young guy I'll someday marry. Will I be good enough? I don't want to tell him. Richard is trying to help me block, or at least dim, even the past thoughts in my mind, but it's not all that easy. They're like little hot coals popping out of a fire at the most unsuspecting times. Once I was rocking their baby and pretending that it was my own, and that I was married to Mr. Nice and waiting for him to come home from work and all that, and it was like my mental computer doors fell off—everything in every little detail from my past flooded out all over me. I quick put the baby back in his bed so he wouldn't be contaminated. That was one hard night to get through.

Richard is trying to teach me that everyone has the right to choose for themselves, and that I mustn't be so condemning of fruits, fairies, queers, yucks . . . shits . . . filths . . . and anything else I can call them; and I am trying, I really am trying to let everybody live their own lives just as I wish they had let me live mine. But I'm still filled, maybe even sometimes obsessed, with hatred for that filthy teacher pig that sucked me into her weirdo culture. If dirty old adults want to practice weird things in their locked back rooms, that's one thing, but trying to sell all the kids in the world on their sick culture is . . . just that . . . shit . . . throw up . . . vomit . . . I can't think of enough bad words.

Do I worry if I'll ever go back? No! No way! I'll become a nun before I'll ever slip to that depth again. It isn't just that their acts are with the same sex, it's that most of them are so promiscuous, so . . .

I'm sorry, I don't want to talk about it any more, it's too heavy. Actually I'm out of it now anyway. I've started a new, happy, straight life. I've got lots of friends here at Happy House, real friends who once had problems, too. We never talk about their problems, just try to reenforce each other's strengths.

It was really strange when Mom first found I was going there, how uptight and on the rag she got. She couldn't figure out why I'd want to hang around a bunch of "losers" like that. At least she couldn't until I lied and told her it was an assignment for my psychology class. That she believed!

Or maybe it was just what she wanted to hear. Parents are so funny. But I do love her, and as I get older, I more and more appreciate how hard it is to raise a kid in a one-parent home. Believe me, my kids won't be raised like that. I'm going to know and care about every move they make; no . . . they wouldn't like that either; everyone has to have a certain amount of freedom, but they need love and caring, too. I think love and caring first, and with enough of it most of the other problems can be ironed out, right?

Aren't you proud I've made it back? I'm proud of myself, too. But the scars are still there. Man, how I wish those scars would go away.

JANE—about peer pressure

Oh wow! I didn't think I'd ever see you again. Sure, I'd like to go out to lunch with you. Meet you in front at one minute after twelve.

Do I like being a beauty operator? Not especially, but I blew the education bit by trying to be so "with-it" when I was young, with something, but against myself and everything I loved and respected.

Actually, working here isn't really all that bad. I make pretty good money as a beauty operator, and in June I'm going to marry a really neat guy, who has two-and-a-half more years of college. I'll work to put him through; then stop and hopefully become a Mother, two, three, or four times.

Sometimes I feel bad that I'm such a rotten speller and know so little about all the things I should have been learning and could have learned if I'd only been listening and trying in school, but I'm taking two night classes at the junior college near here—dumbbell English and math. The math is solely for challenge. It's always been my hardest subject and the one I thought I hated the most; so I'm taking it strictly for discipline. I think in some ways that was the thing that got me into trouble the most—no discipline, insisting upon doing only what I wanted to do, never what I *should* have been doing! Not wanting anyone, anytime, anywhere telling me what to do! For a few years there I couldn't stand having my teachers, my parents—anybody—tell me anything; in fact it just made me want even more to do the exact opposite. I can't believe those years were real. I got so far off, so gradually, I never even knew when it happened, but I've changed. I'm in charge of a Big Sister group for little girls who come from problem families, or need help with their social school work, and I've really got my life together. My parents and I are so close I can't believe it. Actually, we always were; they never did let me down. I just let them and myself down.

And I'm not only taking my two night classes and really studying like I never did before in my whole life, but I'm taking piano lessons again just to prove to myself that I can do it! I always had such a poor self-image behind my loud, brassy, show-off exterior. I always thought I was dumb and incapable; actually, I'm sure that over the years all the stupid teachers I had brainwashed me to think of myself as a dumb, I-couldn't-do-it-if-I-tried, incompetent. Thank God for my family. I don't know what kids do who don't have supportive families. Maybe they can handle the system better, but I couldn't. Or maybe that's just another cop-out blaming my weaknesses on the school, but honestly and realistically I do think schools have to take a larger part of the responsibility to groom success kids instead of failure kids. That's what we're trying to do in the Big Brother, Big Sister programs; just teach kids what fantastic winners they really are, and that they can do anything they want to do badly enough if they have the *right peers* and enough self-confidence.

Most of the kids in my old crowd were insecure, rebellious, can't-cooperate-with-anybody losers, like me.

Duke once said he got fed up with our going nowhere thing and decided to go straight. He made an appointment to have his greasy, long hair and beard cut and even bought some new clothes.

231

But that very night his Dad started climbing the walls again about the way he dressed, and his hair and beard and sleazy friends, and he had to give up his whole personal renovation job. He felt it would have made him lose face with himself to do what he really wanted to do under his old man's pressure. I know it doesn't make sense, but it's the way some kids think. That very night Duke started into real heavy doping. About three weeks later he OD'd. I wanted to tell his parents, but I didn't know whether it would make them feel better or worse, more responsible or less, so of course I did nothing.

That was in the olden days when I was completely self-centered, selfish, and unprincipled, as well as had a super, super negative outlook and R.A. (rotten attitude), and a putrid personal profile. Actually, I didn't know how to be happy and at peace with myself and everything and everyone around me. I kind of brought discord and disharmony with me, like the little guy in the comics with the black cloud. I couldn't quite ever get in tune with people, things, or myself. But I have now!

How? Actually, it was very simple. I applied the principles of a "Yes, I Can" class that I took at the college—under much pressure from my Mother, I must admit. When I started looking at myself as I was, as the exact opposite of everything my teacher taught, when I started seeing what a bitch I was and what an R.A. I had, I couldn't believe it.

The first night I went to class knowing I'd hate it and the teacher and everything else. And when she quoted: "Your attitude determines your altitude," I almost got up and walked out. It was an old bromide my Dad was always using. But then she started proving it by a fascinating self-hypnosis demonstration. It wasn't just another dull, dumb lecture class. It had enough thought-transference experiments, and nonverbal language quizzes, and contagious-attitude projects, and meditation workshops that I finally got to know myself. Imagine, I was twenty years old, and I didn't know who I was, not the real me anyway, only the glumpy, globy exterior that had eroded on me in my rotten past.

It was like, little by little, we hacked that crap away in the "Yes, I Can" class, and now I'm so excited about the whole project and the new me. I'm applying it at the children's level to the kids I work with in my Big Sister program. Oh, that's another thing, the old me would no more have gone out of her way for others than anything. Now I'm actually in charge of a group of six Big Sisters as well as having a Little Sister of my own. This is a project through the college where an older girl helps a younger girl, usually a grade school or junior high school kid, with her home-work and maybe music, or sports, or whatever she needs. But mainly we work to get her a good, healthy, sound, strong self-image! We play the part of an extended family giving *positive support* and *reinforcement* and *ever, ever, ever building that fragile ego thing!* We structure *winners!*

When we have our leaders' councils, we some-times report almost miraculous changes in kids. I guess it's the most fulfilling and exciting thing that has ever happened in my complete life—other than my coming marriage, of course.

You want to know about the "Yes, I Can" pro-gram in a nutshell? Well, I know it's going to sound superficial without all the fun personal in-volvement things, and there really isn't anything you haven't heard a million times before, but it's the *doing* that's important! If you don't *do* some-thing about what you know, even knowledge can be a burden.

"Yes, I Can" makes you integrate into your life simple things like learning that all of life is like a rose, which has beauty, fragrance, *and thorns.* People program themselves to see *only* what they're looking for. Some people are always both-ered or inconvenienced or annoyed by the thorns. That was me! I missed entirely the beauty and the fragrance of the rose!

Another thing, no one really appreciates how

susceptible they are to people and things around them. For instance, in class the teacher brought a lemon, cut it in half and slowly sucked the whole thing. By the time she was through, and she hadn't said a word, we were all so puckered up we could hardly believe it when we looked in the mirror. *Homo sapiens* are alarmingly programmed, usually unknowingly, by outside stimuli.

In learning to trust people, we had to gain enough confidence to fall and let someone catch us. That was really hard for me, and I hadn't known how little I trusted people outside my own family.

When I set a goal for myself to go one full day and say only positive things, I couldn't believe how many times I had to bring out the old pad and give myself minus marks. And when I tried to go one day being kind in every action, word, and deed, I didn't want to believe how inconsiderate I really was. When I experimented with appreciation, I found I didn't at all like the stranger who inhabited the inside of my body. This taught me that "Your mind controls your body and you control your mind."

It was really rough, but in six weeks I had made a good start towards molding the new me! It takes six weeks to establish a habit, and I sure had a lot of them to change, but I am changing! I've found that truly, Yes, I can! Yes, everybody can!